It's All in Your Head

Remarkable Facts About the Human Mind

JEAN STINE
and
CAMDEN BENARES

PRENTICE HALL GENERAL REFERENCE
NEW YORK LONDON TORONTO SYDNEY TOKYO SINGAPORE

To my beloved wife, June: companion, lover, friend
CAMDEN BENARES

To the parents who smiled with loving indulgence on the hundreds of books I accumulated in my room as a child: Henry Alfred Stine and Polly Marie Lewis
JEAN STINE

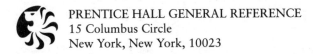 PRENTICE HALL GENERAL REFERENCE
15 Columbus Circle
New York, New York, 10023

Contact Library of Congress for full CIP data.

ISBN: 0-671-85023-7

Designed by Irving Perkins Associates, Inc.

Manufactured in the United States of America

First Edition

10   9   8   7   6   5   4   3   2   1

Acknowledgments

Both authors especially want to thank their estimably patient editor, Deirdre Mullane, and their able agent, Bert Holtje, for their contributions toward making this project a reality.

In addition, Jean Stine wishes to acknowledge:

Janrae Frank, whose heroic efforts alone made this book's publication possible.

Glen Frehey, Eddie and Mary Carvajal, Dianne Wickes, Bobby Armbruster, Jean and Gene Courtney, Jock Root, David Gottleib, Robert Wood, Ken Goldsmith, and David McDaniel, for reasons they know best.

Forrest Ackerman for the moral and financial support for which so many others are equally indebted.

Margaret Davis for teaching me how to squeeze out the fat.

Jeremy Tarcher for pointing the way.

David Edwin Stine and Vic for being quiet so I could finish.

And Mark Demian Stine for providing 200 cups of coffee while we went over the copy-edited manuscript.

And of course the patient staff of the Pasadena and South Pasadena public libraries.

Contents

Introduction

Nothing fascinates us more than ourselves. It's an old truism proven by the thousands of books written about psychology, sexual behavior, and our myriad problems. And few can resist those magazine quizzes that allow us to figure out if we are "normal," or would make good mates, or have a "dynamic" personality.

This fascination can be traced to an age-old human urge to satisfy our curiosity about who we are, what makes us tick, and why others behave as they do. Our curiosity about both ourselves and others arises from a universal need to follow the philosopher's dictate and "know thyself."

Yet for all our obsession with ourselves, we remain ignorant of the most basic facts about our own natures. This lack of knowledge becomes all the more curious when you consider that today we live in the midst of a greater abundance of information about the human mind and how it works than has ever existed before in history. In just the past two decades, specialists have learned as much as they knew altogether before about the brain, personality, motivation, and behavior.

But despite the flood tide of recent research, little of this information trickles down to the average person. Most popular books on psychology are aimed at helping readers overcome specific personal problems—anger, addiction, troubled relationships—or achieve success and sexual fulfillment. A few other ponderous tomes offer overviews of psychology itself or the basic theories of personality. Almost none contain even a smattering of the knowledge researchers have amassed in recent years about the many aspects of the mind and personality. Much of this information remains buried in professional journals representing dozens of disciplines from psychology to anthropology to medicine, neuroanatomy, biochemistry, and endocrinology.

This book aims to fill a tiny portion of that gap. In it you will find more than 400 entries about the human mind and psychology drawn from the cutting edge of research. Each item has been presented both because it is fascinating in its own right and for the insights it offers into our minds and behavior.

Some of these entries will no doubt amuse you; others shock. Some will challenge cultural beliefs; others personal beliefs. But no matter how far out, unlikely, or unpleasant the findings may seem, each is based on solid scientific study. (You'll find a reading list citing most of the books and journals consulted in the preparation of this book at the end.) Nothing in this book is meant to be considered the last word on or a definitive treatment of the subjects covered. There are no last steps in science—only first steps and steps along the way. Nor are there any definitive treatments—no matter how eminent the authority. No matter how many thousands of studies substantiate a "fact"—our bias toward physical attractiveness, for instance—there are always others, equally sound, that seem to contradict it. Sometimes time resolves these disputes—sometimes it only intensifies them.

Most people know very little about the brain—its structure, composition, chemistry, functioning—and nothing about the mind, thought, memory, motivation, intelligence, creativity, performance, therapists, therapy, or mental illness. Did you know, for instance:

- What causes mental illness
- Where our consciousness is located
- The brain mechanisms that allow you to read this page
- The difference between a psychologist and a psychiatrist
- The single greatest factor influencing the success of a marriage

- What causes music, books, and art to "move" us so deeply
- How secondhand cigarette smoke affects our mental and emotional states
- How rock music can help boost memory
- Who is considered the "founder" of psychology
- Why some women and men become addicted to fitness
- About new discoveries like a "peace pill" that inhibits aggressive behavior but doesn't affect the ability to fight back in self-defense
- Why stress can be good for you
- What eye-blinking can tell you about another's thoughts and feelings
- Why the odds are five to one against developing high self-esteem
- How friendships affect health
- The genetic reason why men go to extremes in the arts, crime, and mental illness
- Why we like tall people more than short people
- The 10 things that frighten us most
- Why some children won't play
- Why many bilingual people take on a different personality with each language they speak
- Why we are willing to discuss our night dreams, but reluctant to verbalize our daydreams
- Why men and women's motivations for sex reverse with age
- The percentage of men who cry on the job
- Sigmund Freud's very personal reasons for thinking that sex was the cause of mental illness
- Why older workers can concentrate on the job better than younger ones
- How to become awake and aware in your dreams
- Why therapy works and how to get the most from it

- Why intimacy can be bad for a relationship
- Why more than 70 percent of parents said that if they had the choice to make over again, they wouldn't have children
- What therapists do for you that you can do for yourself
- Why we grow taller or shorter as our mood changes
- Why inner silence promotes physical and mental health
- Why heterosexuals daydream about gay sex and gays fantasize about heterosexual sex
- Why dreams can give early warning of serious illness
- Why men don't have to ask for directions
- Why scientists say there are more than 12 different human genders
- Why women may make "ideal" soldiers
- Just how long is "now"
- The sex link between the brain and the foot
- What pregnant women dream about most, and why
- What three items found in your refrigerator can boost memory, stabilize mood, and ease mental illness
- How you can reset the brain's clock to prevent jet lag

In this book, you'll find theories about what our dreams and fantasies mean; why we think, feel, and do the things we do; how to tell if we're "going crazy"; whether we're "normal" sexually; how much we're in control of our behavior; whether we really become wiser as the years pass; and how we can make relationships work better.

You'll encounter these and other intriguing facts scientists have uncovered about the three-pound universe inside our heads—and about those who seek to help us understand it. You'll discover the newest data about the brain, the mind, intelligence, mood, memory, and thought; how the body affects the mind and how the mind affects the body; therapy, therapists, and their clients; mental health and mental illness; gender, sexuality, mating, and marriage; mental and emotional development from childhood to old age; as well as sleep, work, creativity, dreams, and the conscious and unconscious. Old folk wisdom will be substantiated, cultural myths demolished, and new horizons opened.

You will also discover that many of the founders of psychology led personal lives that seem to make them more fit to be patients than therapists. We are not trying to "bash" these eminent men, but to humanize them, to show that they were as quirky and irrational as the rest of us. In our view, we can only progress as individuals when we understand that humanity triumphs not through the efforts of fortunate individuals more perfect than the rest, but through the efforts of imperfect people like ourselves who see beyond and transcend their own limitations.

You will find an underlying theme in this book. You won't read about "subjects," "patients," or "individuals" here. The authors don't see psychology as being about something that happens to others or to faceless individuals. Psychology is about us—you, me, we, everyone—and what happens to us, why we think what we do, feel what we do, and do what we do.

This book explores a couple of other themes as well. One is that no single theory explains all of our behavior. "In this age of computers and space travel, our understanding of our own mind is as erroneous as the ancients' idea of earth as a flat surface," writes guidance system pioneer Thomas R. Blakeslee. "Just as mankind was fooled for centuries by the obvious flatness of the earth, we have accepted a false understanding of our minds based on what we seem to see clearly when we look at our own thoughts. We have been fooled by a powerful illusion of mental unity into ignoring and misunderstanding the thoughts, knowledge, and emotions of half our brain."

But, Blakeslee contends, "when you look at a human brain, it is difficult to see how people could ever have thought of it as the physical basis of a singular 'mind.' For the brain is clearly a double organ . . . two identical-looking hemispheres joined together by several bundles of nerve fibers."

A deeper examination of the brain would reveal even further

divisions, each a minibrain of its own, fully equivalent to those of many animals. Although these subbrains have a loose working agreement, each has its own job, its own imperatives, its own problems, and its own needs. Throughout our lives, each subbrain clamors to have its own priorities and needs put first. Sometimes one dominates, sometimes another. But there is no one unified thing we can call "the" brain.

Another theme you'll find in these pages is the conviction that the brain is a great deal more than a glorified computer. "More and more it is becoming fashionable to look upon the brain as though it were, in some ways, an immensely complicated computer made up of extremely small switches, the neurons," observes scientist and science writer Isaac Asimov. But, "In comparison," he writes, "the structure of a computer . . . is primitively simple."

According to Asimov, the brain's three pounds contain almost 100 billion cells, each of which is connected to many other nerve cells, creating "a complex pattern that allows the tiny electrical currents that mark nerve action to flow in any of a vast number of possible pathways. No computer yet built, he notes, contains 100 billion "switching units." In addition, "the wiring of the brain is far more complicated than in any computer." And, while the components that make up a computer are "either on or off," Asimov points out, our brain cells are "magnificent objects . . . each undoubtedly . . . more complicated than an entire computer."

All these themes combine to form this book's final theme: It favors a compromise on the question of free will versus determinism. *Free will* is not a term you will find in these pages. We were unable to discover a single reference to the subject among the indexes of the several hundred books and journals we consulted while researching this volume. Instead, most scientific advances into our understanding of the mind seem only to provide further reinforcement for the idea that free will is just an illusion—and the more deterministic and causal our lives appear. Looked at in this way, Nobel laureate neuroscientist Roger Sperry says, the sciences seem to suggest "there is no reason to think that any of us had any real choice to be anywhere else, or even to believe in principle that our presence was not already 'in the cards', so to speak, 5, 10, or 15 years ago."

Sperry notes that he does not feel comfortable with this line of thinking and suspects the reader won't either. In its place, he offers the following persuasive case that if free will didn't exist, the complexity of the brain's structure would have created it. "If you were assigned to design and build the perfect free-will model (let us say the perfect, all-wise, decision-making machine)," he claims, "your aim might . . . be . . . to contact all related information, in proportion—past, present and future."

Strangely, by whatever twist of fate, the human brain has evolved a long way in exactly that direction, Sperry observes. He points out "the amount and kind of factors that this multidimensional intracranial vortex [the brain] draws into itself, scans, and brings to bear on the process of turning out its 'preordained decisions' [include] thanks to memory, the events and collected wisdom of most of a human lifetime." We can also throw into this mix our fluctuating biochemistries, fluctuating circumstances outside us, and "the accumulated knowledge of all recorded history." Then, "we must add to all the foregoing, thanks to reason and logic, much of the future forecast and predictive value extractable from all these data." The final result would have to be "a very long jump in the direction of freedom from the primeval slime mould, the Jurassic sand dollar, or even the latest model orangutan."

Unlike many other books on psychology, this one doesn't promise to make your life better. But, on the other hand, don't be surprised if it does. Although it's not a self-help book, it will probably tell you many things about the mind that will illuminate your own life. Although not a book about the history or development of psychology it may deepen your understanding of both. And although it's not a book about sexual behavior, marriage, or how to find a mate, readers may find they've gained much useful knowledge about these subjects as well.

What you will encounter here is a compendium of intriguing and little-known facts about psychology and the mind. The contents are guaranteed to be thought-provoking, mentally nourishing (sticking to the mind instead of the ribs), and to exceed the recommended minimum daily dosage of food for thought.

The Brain

FACTS AND FIGURES

Melon Head
The human brain is about the size and shape of a ripe cantaloupe.

A Soggy What?
The brain is split down the middle and wrinkled on the outside. It looks a great deal like a soggy, overgrown walnut.

Wrap It Up to Go
The human skull contains slightly over three pounds of gray, viscid brain matter.

Better Than a CD-ROM
Our brains are capable of retaining about 100 billion bits of information. That's the equivalent of 500 encyclopedias.

No Wonder We're So Bright
There are 200 billion neurons in the adult human brain. That's as many stars as there are in some galaxies.

And You Thought the Phone Company Had Problems
When we are thinking, our brain cells can link up with as many as 200,000 others. But the average neuron (brain cell) only connects

with 60,000. Altogether, there are over 100 trillion possible connections within the average brain. No wonder our mental wires get crossed from time to time.

Low Wattage
The brain runs on electricity. But if the brain of the world's greatest genius were hooked up to a socket, it wouldn't generate enough power to light the average light bulb. The total output of the brain is a mere 20 watts!

A Real Energy Saver
A single memory uses one-tenth of the energy contained in a single particle of light.

Not Exactly a Live Wire
The speed of thought isn't that fast. The fastest thoughts in the brain travel at no more than 300 miles per hour. That's far slower than household electricity.

Everything we know about the vast complexities of the universe around us is contained in a grayish pudding of brain cells that weighs about three pounds. This has led some scientists and journalists to dub our brain "the three-pound universe."

Talk About Getting a Swelled Head!
The brain triples in size from birth to maturity. But from adulthood to old age, it shrinks by more than an ounce.

No Wonder We're Tired
As we think, the brain undergoes 100,000 chemical interactions per second.

Best One-Line Description of the Brain
"The brain is a little saline pool that acts as a conductor, and it runs on electricity."—Hooper and Teresi, *3-Pound Universe*

A Short Tour of the Brain
The brain and its connections are so complex that no one function is located in a single spot. Different portions of the brain process and store the same experience simultaneously. But scientists agree on the following, which includes the principal parts of the brain and their primary functions:

Brain-stem. The body's transatlantic cable, carries signals from the senses to the brain and from the brain back to the body.

Cerebellum. The body's drill sergeant, coordinates muscle movement and keeps the higher portions of the brain informed of the motion of fingers, legs, and feet.

Limbic system. The brain's morale officer, controls learning and motivation through coordinating sensory data with basic bodily needs like hunger and sex. The limbic system consists of a number of subsystems, each with specific tasks:

· **Hypothalamus.** The brain's taskmaster, uses pleasure and pain to regulate the state of the body, temperature, and hunger.
· **Thalamus.** The brain's administrative assistant, passes data from the senses to the cortex.
· **Basal ganglia.** The brain's acrobat, coordinates balance and the movement of the body.
· **Hippocampus.** The brain's receptionist, holds short-term memory and passes it to other parts of the brain for permanent storage.
· **Amygdala.** The brain's data transfer system, relays memories and habits from storage in the subconscious to consciousness in the cortex

Cortex. The brain's brain and its uppermost layer, center of intelligence, thought, memory, decision making, and voluntary action. Like the limbic system, the cortex is actually a complex of organs, all working together but each with its own assigned tasks:

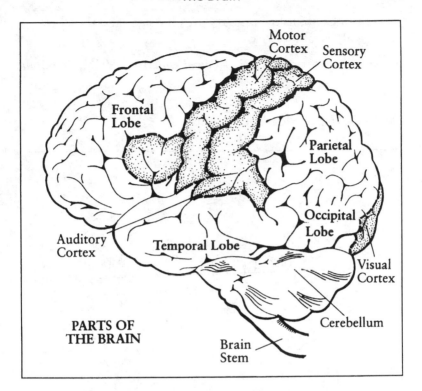

Motor Cortex
Sensory Cortex
Frontal Lobe
Parietal Lobe
Occipital Lobe
Auditory Cortex
Temporal Lobe
Visual Cortex
Cerebellum
PARTS OF THE BRAIN
Brain Stem

· **Frontal lobes** (or neocortex). The brain's CEO (lies behind the forehead), its newest and most highly developed function. The true center of personality and thought. Processes the future, plans in advance, and looks beyond the self for the good of others and the group.

· **Parietal lobes.** The brain's president (arches over the brain from ear to ear). Center for sense of touch, determines which incoming information should receive the highest priority.

· **Temporal lobe.** The brain's audio system (behind both temples). The center for hearing and the coordination of sight with sound.

· **Occipital lobe.** The brain's video system (back of

head). Contains the primary area for sight and the storage of visual memory.

SOURCE: Hooper and Teresi, *3-Pound Universe*; Asimov, *The Brain*.

The Little Men Inside Your Brain

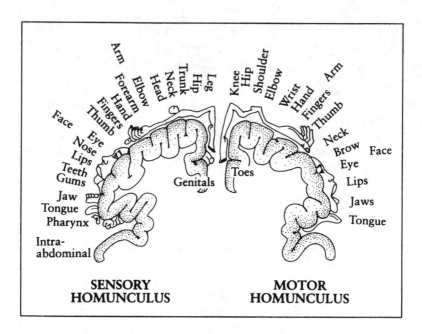

SENSORY HOMUNCULUS   **MOTOR HOMUNCULUS**

There are two little "men" inside our brains. Scientists call them the sensory and motor homunculi (*homunculus* means "little man"). Each is an inch-by-inch representation of the human senses. Each area of the sensory homunculus receives sensations from a specific part of the body: torso, legs, arms, fingers, nostrils, eyes, lips, and tongue. Each area of the motor homunculus sends signals back to one of those bodily parts.

The brain's map of the body is distorted: According to their importance to the brain, we would have oversize tongues, lips, genitals, fingers, and eyes. Neuroanatomists explain that this is because supersensitive body parts, and those requiring extreme physical coordination, take up more brain cells. An inch of tongue sends back signals to a much wider area of a homunculus than an inch of the back.

If our homunculi could be photographed, here is what we would see: Two little men, their toes tucked into the cleft between the lobes in front of the cerebellum, stretching backward around the cortex away from each other with elongated legs and trunks, small heads, and enormous fingers. Beyond their tiny heads, about midway around (roughly where our temples are), you would see two separate enormous faces with immense eyes, lips, tongues, and noses.

SOURCE: Campbell, *Musical Brain*.

Brain Dead

All the privileges of being an adult are bestowed upon us when we turn twenty-one. But crepe should be the order of the day, not celebration. For the ripe old age of twenty-one marks a more sobering turning point. It's also the age at which we begin losing our minds—or at least our brain cells. You can bid good-bye to more than 10,000 brain cells every morning after the age of twenty-one.

That may sound like a lot, but it's merely 70,000 per week, or an insignificant 3.5 million per year. During the rest of your life, you'll only lose 200 million brain cells. So relax, you won't miss them. With some 200 billion brain cells packed in your cranium, that's less than 1 percent of the total. You've still got plenty of brain power to spare.

SOURCE: Asimov, *The Brain*.

Permanent Waves

Most of us think of sleep, normal waking consciousness, intense creativity, and quiet relaxation as completely different. But new understanding of brain waves suggests these four states are more closely related than we realize. By listing brain waves in alphabetical order, most charts obscure a number of surprising relationships that only become apparent when brain waves are arranged in terms of increasing frequency (cycles per second or CPS) instead.

- **Delta waves** (1–3 CPS) signify we have fallen into a deep dreamless sleep.
- **Theta waves** (4–7 CPS) generated only during great stress or emotion and intense creativity.
- **Alpha waves** (8–12 CPS) appear when we feel relaxed, rested, daydreamy.
- **Beta waves** (18–40 CPS) produced during normal, everyday awareness and when we are dreaming

Seen this way, it is obvious that sleeping, intense emotional states, and relaxation—which feel so different to us—each begin where the other ends. The jump of 6 CPS—almost as many CPS as the width of any two other wave bands combined—between relaxation and the beta state suggests the brain has to generate twice as much energy to make the leap from relaxed awareness to alert concentration.

The fact that delta and theta waves lie side by side also suggests a closer link between where our heads are at during intense emotional states and creativity and where they are at during sleep than was previously suspected. Another surprising fact is that daydreaming is more closely related to creativity than to sleep.

SOURCE: Campbell, *Musical Brain.*

Not Easily Shocked

Brain tissue is extremely delicate, not much thicker than oatmeal. Unprotected, the slightest touch or jar could injure it seriously. So nature has given our brain cells their own built-in shock absorber.

The outermost layer of this shock absorber is the skull. Rap on it with your knuckles, and you will feel, for all its lightness, how strong and resilient its bones are. Beneath this protective shell are three layers of membranes that further cushion the brain from shock and injury.

Just inside the skull is a shock-absorbent coating of tough, fibrous membranes (the *dura mater* or "hard mother"). Below the dura mater is a thin, weblike tissue that acts as a second layer of protection (the *arachnoid* or "cobwebs"). Through these, the brain is anchored to the skull by a delicate membrane (*pia mater* or "tender mother").

Between the pia mater and the arachnoid is a clear, colorless liquid (cerebrospinal fluid) that surrounds the brain, serving as a last line of defense in shielding our oh-so-sensitive brains.

SOURCE: *Compton's Encyclopedia.*

The Holes in Your Head

The most important part of the brain is not the cells, but the gaps between them, called synapses. What takes place in our synapses determines an enormous amount about us: personality, memory, mood, mental and physical health, intelligence, and even the ability to love and mate. According to the authors of *3-Pound Universe*, the gaps between our cells are the critical juncture where many of the fundamental decisions in our brains are made.

When our brain cells originate or pass on a signal, they send an electrical charge to the edge of the cell where it triggers the release of a chemical messenger known as a neurotransmitter. The neurotransmitter crosses the gap (the synaptic cleft) to the next cell, where it releases an electrical charge that carries the message inward.

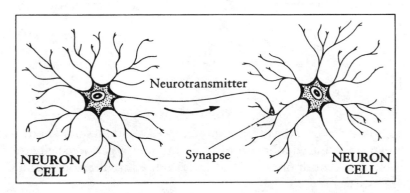

Neurotransmitter

NEURON CELL   Synapse   NEURON CELL

But many things can happen to a neurotransmitter during its 0.3 millisecond to 1.0 millisecond voyage across the synaptic cleft. A crossing signal or chemical fluctuation can break it down in the gap before it reaches the other cell; the other cell can even refuse to accept the signal. In both cases the result is the same as if no signal were transmitted at all.

When a message successfully passes all the synaptic clefts between it and its destination, a thought may be generated, a muscle contracted, a mood-altering hormone secreted, or the functioning of our nervous system or organs affected. Ultimately, every aspect of who we are and what we do is determined by what transpires in these gaps. Many neurobiologists believe that the mysterious source of personality and behavior lies here, in the holes in our heads.

SOURCE: Hooper and Teresi, *3-Pound Universe.*

BRAIN MATTER

It Never Sleeps

Whether we are awake or asleep, at any given moment millions of our brain cells are at work. Twenty-four hours a day, seven days a week, information is being fed into the cerebrum and signals are sent back out to the body. Even when we sleep, our nervous system is constantly relaying information on the position of our limbs, the temperature of our body, and all the thousands of individual activities involved in breathing, digesting, and dreaming. No wonder we wake up so tired every morning.

SOURCE: Asimov, *The Brain.*

Your Brain Breathes

To do all its work, the brain needs oxygen. We've all said, I need a breather! or I need a breath of fresh air! after a period of intense mental concentration. But it's not us that needs to breathe, it's our brains.

In directing your thinking, sensing, and movements, the brain consumes more than a quarter of the body's oxygen. Intense mental concentration depletes as much oxygen and energy as intense physical exercise. After a while, the oxygen levels in the blood begin to fall and the brain begins to crave more oxygen than we can get sitting in a room thinking, so it signals us to stand up, stretch, move around, and go for a walk. Your brain wants a breather.

SOURCE: Ibid.

It Makes You Smarter

On the other hand, exercise can increase the amount of oxygen reaching our brains by as much as 30 percent. Studies have shown that increasing the amount of oxygen available to the brain increases mental activity. Jogging, a brisk walk, or mowing the lawn can restore your mental edge.

SOURCE: Ibid.

No Harder Than Goofing Off

People who are mentally lethargic often use the excuse, Thinking makes me tired. Now Allan Gevins, director of EEG Systems Laboratory, says they're right. It takes just as much energy to scribble mindlessly as it does to paint a masterpiece.

Gevins used an eight-channel EEG to record the brain waves of people engaged in serious drawing and those who were just doodling. He had expected to find that those who were concentrating on what they were doing would generate more mental energy than the doodlers. But to his surprise, Gevins discovered that both activities took the same amount of energy. One researcher suggested that since you have to generate just as much energy to goof off as you do to paint a masterpiece, you might as well just paint a masterpiece.

SOURCE: Alan Gevins, "Electrical Potentials in Human Brain During Cognition," *Science*, August 21, 1981.

Blindsight

Some people who lose their sight due to a stroke or brain injury develop an amazing ability. Although unable to physically see an object placed before them, they are able to reach out unerringly and touch it with a sureness that confounds researchers. The term coined for this ability is *blindsight*.

Psychologist Anthony Marcel of Cambridge University has studied blindsight for two decades. His discoveries show that blindsight occurs only when the injury is confined to those areas of the brain involved in transmitting visual signals and not the neural areas that receive and interpret the signals. Although what the subjects see is no longer transmitted to the portion of the brain that does the "seeing," the message from their visual centers is still being transmitted below the level of their awareness (the subconscious) to other portions of the brain. These parts of the brain know where the object is, allowing someone with blindsight to reach out and touch it on the first attempt.

The phenomenon of blindsight tells us that one part of the mind may not know what the other part is doing.

SOURCE: Hooper and Teresi, *3-Pound Universe*.

Self-Repairing

Scientists say the ideal machine would sense when it is going out of whack and replace the affected parts itself. Once built, it would run for years without ever needing to be repaired. Researchers at the University of California at San Francisco, however, have already discovered such a machine: the human brain.

Neuroscientists were put on the trail by the "phantom limb" phenomenon. People who had lost limbs told doctors they could "still feel" the missing limb. At the time, scientists believed that the brain cells controlling a body part died when that part was amputated. They assumed that sensations in phantom limbs resulted from stimulation of nerves near where the limb had been severed.

Current research reveals that the brain does not have fixed circuits. Instead, it appears to be capable of reorganizing itself over incredibly large distances, so that, for example, brain cells receiving input from the face and shoulder can trigger brain cells no longer receiving input from an arm. Once we learn how the brain manages this rewiring, it should be possible to help the process along. This offers great hope to many people suffering from nervous-system disorders, spinal cord injury, paralysis, stroke, depression, mental illness, and brain injury.

SOURCE: Sandra Blakeslee, "Missing Limbs, Still Atingle, Clues to Changes in the Brain," *New York Times*, November 10, 1992.

The Brain's Own Microwave Receiver

Could the benign and ubiquitous microwave have a sinister side? Could all those cellular phones, power lines, satellite dishes, and even the wiring in your house, have an effect on the brain? Neuroscientist W. Ross Adey believes they might. Disturbing research he performed at the Pettis Memorial Veterans Administration Hospital, Loma Linda, California, proved our brains—and our minds—respond strongly to surrounding electromagnetic fields.

Adey found that brain cells synchronize their firing to surrounding microwaves. In one experiment, an excited monkey calmed down and began to produce alpha waves when a carefully modulated electromagnetic field was broadcast at it. Adey calls the microwave's ability to alter mood and mental functioning a bit ominous in a world where there is no escape from electromagnetic fields.

But relax. If Adey were right, our cities (which are saturated by electromagnetic fields) would be full of the mentally disturbed—and we all know that's not so.

SOURCE: Hooper and Teresi, *3-Pound Universe*.

Brain Food

Looking for uppers, downers, sleeping pills, painkillers, or memory enhancers? Forget the corner drugstore. Tomorrow's highs—as well as the chemicals that will help boost intelligence, stabilize moods, and ease mental illness—will come out of your refrigerator. MIT neuroendocrinologist Richard Wurtman has massed an impressive collection of evidence demonstrating that the brain's vital neurotransmitter levels are determined by what we eat. Eggs, liver, and soybeans are rich in the neurotransmitter acetylcholine. Proteins contain the amino acids, tyrosine and tryptophan—all involved in the building of norepinephrine, one of the brain's prime memory boosters. So whether you are a vegetarian or a meat eater, enhanced memory, mood, and mental function are no farther away than your local grocery.

SOURCE: Ibid.

The Dirty Brained

Scientists have traced responsibility for many of our abilities and facilities to specific areas in the brain. Now neuroanatomists may have located the site where our ability to use dirty words is located. When this area is damaged, victims can suffer from an uncontrollable compulsion to utter obscenities. Scatological terms, profanities, and obscenities pour forth in an endless stream. Psychiatrists call this Gilles de la Tourette's syndrome (named after the physician who first identified it). Some people are dirty minded, but these poor souls are clearly dirty brained.

SOURCE: Sagan, *Dragons of Eden*.

Still Room for Improvement

Most of us assume that the human brain is the crown of creation. But the brain took its present form some 40,000 years ago, according to anthropologists. And it hasn't made noticeable progress since.

"We often lose sight of the fact that the brains we carry in our heads are not the last word in nervous systems," warns neurophysiologist Daniel Robinson. We take for granted that a dog's perceptions are limited by its level of evolution, but never consider how limited our own perceptions might be. We accept that dogs are color-blind and can't see the wavelengths that carry colors, but we forget the myriad hues of the wavelengths our eyes can't detect. Perhaps the limitations of our brain structure and chemistry prevent us from perceiving and solving critical problems that would be child's play to a more evolved species.

SOURCE: Robinson, *Enlightened Machine.*

Guess Who's in Charge

People have long wondered who's in charge, the brain or the mind. Is it one of those chicken and egg things that can never be answered?

Neurophysiologists Benjamin Libet and Bertram Feinstein of Mount Zion Hospital in San Francisco believe their research into the mechanisms behind our response to touch may supply a clue.

Women and men were wired up to EEGs and asked to press a button the instant they felt themselves being touched. The results were startling. EEG measurements showed the brain registered the touch in only one ten-thousandth of a second. Participants' fingers signaled this reaction a tenth of a second later by pushing the button. But to Libet and Feinstein's astonishment, the participants themselves were not consciously aware of the touch or of pressing the button until almost a full half-second later.

These results told the researchers two things. First, the decision to push the button was made by the patient's brain, not by his or her mind. For it occurred long before the mind was even aware of the body's having been touched. Second, all the study participants believed they had consciously decided to push the button. Apparently the brain has ways to convince the mind that it is making the decisions—but the brain is definitely in charge.

SOURCE: Talbot, *Holographic Universe.*

Don't Reset Your Clock, Reset Your Brain

Flying to a different time zone, the switch to and from daylight savings time, or a new job schedule can throw off our body's internal rhythms for weeks. We may find ourselves waking when we should be sleeping, wanting breakfast when it's dinnertime, or experiencing a lull in attention just when we most need to be alert. When this happens, we speak of "jet lag" and "the body clock" being off. But it's the brain's clock that's off, not the body's.

Science may be on the way to producing the first jet lag pill. The body's clock resides in the suprachiasmatic nucleus, a small group of brain cells whose nerve fibers are directly linked with the retina, keeping the body locked in rhythm with the pattern of light and dark outside. The suprachiasmatic nucleus is controlled by a hormone called *melatonin*. Dubbed the "Dracula hormone," melatonin floods the body when we are exposed to darkness and puts us to sleep; it is inhibited during daylight, allowing us to wake.

Pioneer sleep researcher Alfred J. Lewy found he could reliably advance or delay a person's biological clock by giving him or her a precisely measured dose of melatonin. Lewy pronounced the results "dramatic." Without competition from daylight, the researchers showed that melatonin pills could readily adjust anyone's biological clock.

SOURCE: Jane E. Brody, "Doses of Pineal Gland Hormone Can Reset Body's Daily Clock," *New York Times*, October 3, 1992.

THE BRAIN-MIND CONNECTION

The Creature with Three Brains

We share our minds with reptiles, mammals, and apes, according to Dr. Paul MacLean, chief of the Brain Evolution and Behavior Laboratory at the National Institute of Mental Health. MacLean sees the brain as divided into three distinct systems, each representing a different stage in our evolution. He dubbed these systems the reptilian, mammalian, and primate brains.

The reptilian brain—the oldest and lowest part of the brain—consists of the brain stem and allied organs. It is ruled by all of the primitive functions and concerns of our reptilian ancestors, including physical space, basic survival, possessions, and the urges of self-defense.

The mammalian brain, the next major development in brain evolution, is also known as the midbrain or limbic system. It performs functions vital to our mammalian ancestors, including memory, learning, emotions, social and family interaction, rewards, and punishments.

The primate brain, the last of our brain systems to develop, consists of the cortex and cerebellum (the frontal lobes). It performs the functions our primate ancestors relied upon for their survival: reasoning things out and trying different solutions.

MacLean believes the brain's triune design has an inherent serious, sometimes catastrophic, "design error." Conflict often develops between the urges and needs of our three brains, between reason and survival and emotion. Dr. MacLean feels this helps explain the "split" we so often feel between reason (the primate brain), instinct (the reptilian brain), and emotion (the mammalian brain), and the difficulty we have resolving it.

SOURCE: Campbell, *Musical Brain*.

I'm of Two Minds About It

Torn between conflicting impulses, most of us have said I'm of two minds about it. Scientists may now have discovered the reason we feel this way so often.

The most noticeable visual feature of the brain is the division running down the middle that separates it into right and left halves (lobes). Neuropsychologists have spent decades charting these two lobes and have found that, although there is some overlap, each processes and responds to different types of information in different ways. Most activities involving speech, language, logic, mathematics, and time sense take place in the left lobe. Activities involving visual and spatial factors, creativity, patterns, inspiration, geometry, and the subconscious take place in the right lobe. These discoveries led to a vogue for the terms "left brain" and "right brain"—which seem to have entered the language via hundreds of pop science books and articles.

For the 95 percent of the population that is right-handed, the two lobes of the brain generally process information in these contrasting modes:

Left Hemisphere	Right Hemisphere
Time	Space
Reason	Emotion
Timed	Timeless
Words	Sounds
Parts	Whole
Analytical thought	Intuitive knowledge
Details	Patterns
Numbers	Geometry
Conscious	Subconscious
Literal	Metaphoric
Specific	General
Speech	Vision

Since both halves of our brain react to a situation, we simultaneously experience two completely opposite perceptions, interpretations, and responses. This may be why we so often feel we are of two minds about a subject.

SOURCE: Ibid.

The Three-Pound Hologram

No need to visit a museum to see a display of holograms. Stanford University neurobiologist Karl Pribram says you've already got a three-pound hologram—in your head.

The theory that the brain operates on holographic principles has gained wide support in the scientific community, since it seems to provide answers to two key questions that have baffled researchers for years:

- What accounts for the survival of learning and memory even after catastrophic injuries?
- How does the mind fuse newly experienced events with earlier memories in the process of learning?

Your high school graduation ceremony is not stored at a specific location, like papers in a file, where it can easily be destroyed. Instead, specific memories are stored *throughout* the brain, just as each portion of a hologram stores the entire image. Because our recollections are so widely spread, they survive and can be retrieved even when we suffer extensive damage to the cells responsible for a specific memory. Holographic storage would also explain how old and new memories merge to produce learning and personality, since each new memory is stored on top of (or within) every preceding memory.

But we have it backward if we believe the brain is like a hologram, Pribram observes. The hologram is actually like the brain. We discovered the principles of holography precisely because they are so much like the way our minds work.

SOURCE: Karl Pribram, "Behaviorism, Phenomenology, and Holism in Psychology," *Journal of Social and Biological Structures*, Vol. 2, 1979.

BEYOND THE BRAIN

An Open Letter

Think you're in touch with reality? Think again. Science says the world you see, taste, feel, smell, and hear is not the real world. It's not even a good simulation.

The colors, sounds, flavors, and scents carried to us by our senses are not straightforward copies of the universe beyond our skin. At best, they are abstractions relayed from our nerve endings in a series of electrical impulses and decoded in a series of complex mathematical operations by our brains. Reality, if we could actually perceive it, would be a rainbow-hued pattern of uncountable interwoven waves: sound waves, gravity waves, and electromagnetic waves. Every object and living creature in the universe is a bundle of radiating energies. We humans are able to see, hear, taste, and smell only the most minute fraction of this spectrum.

As British neuropsychologist Richard Gregory puts it, "Brain states represent the world rather as a letter . . . represents the truth." If so, the real question may be, what kind of letter? A love letter? A Dear John (or Jane) letter? Hate mail? Or just plain junk mail?

SOURCE: Hooper and Teresi, *3-Pound Universe.*

Your Brain's Filter

You've probably changed your car's filter, but what about your brain's filter? Brain mechanics say the brain comes equipped with a filter just as automobiles do. And this filter keeps the brain from clogging up and breaking down, so to speak.

No one can digest the billions of bits of information pouring in from half a trillion brain and nerve cells all at once. The brain's filter prevents overload by determining the most important signals to send straight to conscious awareness, shunting the rest for storage into the subconscious. If this filter were to break down, as happens when the brain is injured or under the influence of psycho-active drugs, we'd be overwhelmed by a flood of sensations. Our ability to sort, remember, and perceive would be so thoroughly short-circuited that afterward we would be unable to recall the experience.

SOURCE: Calder, *Mind of Man*; Hooper and Teresi, *3-Pound Universe.*

How the Mind Works

Many of us take ourselves for granted. We exist, and we rarely reflect on what "we" are or how it is possible for a personal "I" to exist. The mind's greatest mystery, which has long puzzled scientists, is why we are conscious and how our sense of personal consciousness is created. Though scientists have resolved many key questions about how the brain works, the mystery of how the brain creates the mind still remains a subject for heated debate. The front-runners in this controversy are:

The brain site theory. Attempts to explain consciousness by locating the specific sites responsible for each of its individual functions.

The cause and effect theory. Views consciousness as a mere cause and effect reaction to outside stimuli.

The mental monitor theory. Consciousness is simply a system the brain evolved for monitoring the efficiency of its own activities: alertness, perception, memory, movement, decisions, planning, and imagination.

The CEO in your brain theory. Consciousness arose as an executive control function, to help the brain make more sophisticated choices and decisions.

The white noise theory. The randomness of brain impulses (scientists refer to it as mental "white noise") generates personality and consciousness; if every "input" resulted in a fixed "output," we would be computers, incapable of a new response or individuality.

The emergent properties theory. Consciousness is a unique mental function that arose spontaneously as the brain's various subsystems continued to evolve and interact.

The "overlap" theory. Our conscious minds inhabit a moving slot of time 6 to 12 seconds long in which our impressions of the moments just past and of those just to come are overlapped with our experience of the present; it is this critical tenth of a minute that allows us to learn, think, remember, and perceive; without it, we would be unaware of anything more than the present moment, and the world around us would appear random and chaotic.

SOURCE: John Boslough, "The Enigma of Time," *National Geographic*, March 1990.

Personality: It's (Almost) All in Your Head

Where does personality come from? What makes some of us act one way and some another?

The interplay of unique aspects of our backgrounds, behavior, and personality, along with all the learning, reacting, feeling, and experiences we've accumulated in our lifetime, have a lot to do with making us who and what we are. But brain researchers now believe that important building blocks of personality are determined by the way we respond to stimuli, according to science writer Nigel Calder.

Some brains are highly reactive to outside stimuli; others are very sluggish. This phenomenon may lie at the root of two of the most basic types of personality: the extrovert and the introvert. We often think of these as type A and type B personalities, or leaders and followers, or extremely active and extremely passive people. Brain researchers theorize that the extrovert is simply someone whose brain is less easily aroused and requires constant sensory input to keep it active. On the other hand, the brains of introverts may be too easily aroused, even by normal amounts of stimuli, sending them fleeing in search of quiet environments that offer minimal sensory input.

If true, this theory would supply the first strong connection between brain mechanisms and personality.

SOURCE: Calder, *Mind of Man.*

Mind and Memory

Building Blocks

All the art, anguish, science, achievement, passion, poetry, war, selflessness, criminality, and philosophy produced by the human mind are the result of the interaction of five basic functions of the brain:

- Perception
- Emotion
- Thought
- Communication
- Memory

It is to these five faculties that we owe everything, from the sublime genius of Shakespeare to the horror of war and the passion of romantic love.

SOURCE: McWhirter and McWhirter, *Illustrated Encyclopedia.*

PERCEPTION

How You Are Able to Read This Book

How do our minds see? To what do we owe the miraculous gift of sight? Current research says we owe it all to three kinds of cells, each responsible for a specific area of our visual field.

As you read down this page, different groups of brain cells called *feature detectors*, take up the task of registering the page's edge. Turn the book slightly, clockwise or counterclockwise, and completely different groups of feature detectors will begin registering the edges of the page, as it moves into their area of the visual field.

Your ability to see the letters that make up the words on this page is due to these feature detectors, highly specialized cells that recognize the horizontal, vertical, or oblique lines and features of an object. David Hubel and Torsten Weisel, who are responsible for most of our knowledge of how the brain's visual cortex works, have identified three types of feature detector cells: simple, complex, and hypercomplex.

There are three kinds of simple cells, each registering to a specific type of line or feature, although the cell will stop responding if a line is rotated as little as 5 or 10 degrees.

Types of lines that simple cells respond to are:

- A bright line in a specific location in your visual field and sloping in a specific direction.
- A dark line in a specific location in your visual field, sloping in a specific direction.
- A straight edge between a dark and light area in a specific location in your visual field, sloping in a specific direction.

There are also three kinds of complex cells, each recognizing a bright line or bar or edge with a specific slope, regardless of its location in your visual field. As you shift your eyes back and forth while reading this sentence, the same groups of complex cells will continue to register the edges of the page, even though where the edges lie in your visual field may change.

Hypercomplex cells recognize even more subtle features. An individual cell might be conditioned to respond optimally only to a letter of a specific shape and size, moving across your visual field from right to left, but not from left to right.

Together, the hundreds of millions of feature receptors in the visual cortex are responsible for your ability to read all written words.

SOURCE: David Hubel and Torsten Weisel, "Brain Mechanisms of Vision," *Scientific American*, September 1979.

Limited Vision

Research into feature receptors may shed light on a recent discovery by UCLA psychopharmacologist Ronald Siegel: For all their seeming visual and imaginative complexity, our minds produce an astonishingly limited number of visions.

Siegel collected data from thousands of people who had hallucinated as a result of hyperventilation, hypoglycemia, hypnosis, marathon running, the influence of psychedelics, dreaming, daydreaming, sensory bombardment, sensory deprivation, and more than a dozen other altered states of consciousness. Then graphic artists drew the visions that those who Siegel called his "psychonauts" described. Though individual details of their hallucinations differed, the subjects kept "seeing" the same four basic geometric forms: the spiral, the tunnel (or funnel), the cobweb, and the lattice (or honeycomb).

It may be that these visions are hardwired into our visual cortex, the basic shapes our feature receptors recognize and respond to, and the building blocks of our ability to "see" the multitude of complex shapes we perceive in the world around us.

SOURCE: Ronald Siegel, "Hallucinations," *Scientific American*, October 1977.

What Sounds Yellow?

We take our senses pretty much for granted. Seeing is seeing, hearing is hearing. We even have a saying, Seeing is believing. But sometimes, Seeing is hearing.

Our sensory circuits can get crossed like telephone lines. When that happens, we begin to "hear" colors and "see" sounds.

Scientists call this phenomenon synesthesia. It can occur as the result of a bump on the head, damage to the brain, ingesting psychedelic drugs, or spontaneously, without any prior warning.

In auditory-visual synesthesia, the most common form, sounds are seen as colors, as if the person had a "light show" in his or her head. Oddly, human speech, especially vowel sounds, evokes the most vivid visual responses. Higher and shorter vowels are seen as light, bright colors, while longer vowels are perceived as darker, more somber hues. For some reason, yellow is produced by the very short, sharp vowels in the words, *bait* and *beets*.

SOURCE: Hooper and Teresi, *3-Pound Universe*.

The Touch of the Beholder

Science has long acknowledged the truth in the old adage, Beauty is in the eye of the beholder. How we see those we love is influenced more by how we feel about them than by how they actually look. Now there is evidence that how things feel is in the touch of the beholder.

Physiologist Andrea Gwosdow and engineer Larry Berglund, both of Yale University, asked people to rate the feel of a variety of fabrics under various environmental conditions. The way fabrics felt to participants turned out to be strongly influenced by their emotional state. Love, obsession, depression, joy, and delight alter the chemistry throughout the brain and body, according to biological psychiatrist Arnold Mandell, changing "how food tastes, whether music seems pretty, how a person walks . . . his dreams, his body temperature, his appetite, whether he asks for a raise or a vacation."

SOURCE: Holly Hall, "The Feel of Fabric," *Psychology Today*, July 1987.

Where There's Smoke, There's Less Mental Fire

Political decisions are often made in "smoke-filled rooms." Perhaps that's why our political system has reached such a sorry condition. Cigarette smoke does more than clog our lungs, it clogs our wits as well.

Experimenters at Bemidji State University in Minnesota discovered that inhaling someone else's cigarette smoke reduces your alertness, perception, and ability to think clearly. Participants forced to breathe secondhand smoke grew so distracted and irritated that they no longer paid as much attention to events and people around them. In fact, workers in a smoke-filled room were 40 percent less likely to notice—and therefore offer assistance—when someone dropped papers on the floor.

There's an upside to these findings: bosses who learn of them may expect 40 percent greater efficiency, intelligence, and productivity from those working in smokeless offices.

SOURCE: "Smoke Gets In the Way," *Psychology Today*, November 1988.

EMOTIONS

Hard of Feeling

I don't want to hear it! is a common reaction to bad news. Apparently this statement is true literally as well as figuratively. We actually don't hear unpleasant words as well as we do pleasant ones.

Experimenters at the Cambridge University Applied Psychology Research Unit have discovered some words are so highly charged we don't want to hear about them, much less feel the emotions associated with them. They asked people to write down words played on a tape recorder in a noisy room. Participants had significantly more trouble correctly hearing emotionally loaded words like *death* and *blood* than they did hearing neutral words like *square* and *run*.

SOURCE: Calder, *Mind of Man*.

Pity the Lovelorn Cockroach

Emotions are universal. Every living creature feels emotion, says neuroscientist Candace Pert, even cockroaches. "They have to," according to Pert, "because they have chemicals that put them in the mood to mate and chemicals that make them run away when they're about to be killed. That's what emotions are usually about: sex and violence, pain and pleasure. Even bacteria have a little hierarchy of primitive likes and dislikes." If sex is a chemical lure, as Pert claims, it might explain why roaches and politicians have both come to grief after entering their respective motels.

SOURCE: Hooper and Teresi, *3-Pound Universe.*

The Most Emotional Animal

Ever feel your emotions are getting the best of you? You're not alone. Almost everyone feels that way sometimes. It's a natural part of our evolutionary heritage. Humans are the most emotional animals of all, according to Canadian psychologist Donald Hebb.

He believes that as animals evolve and become more intelligent, they become more emotional. Rats are capable of fear; dogs can feel fear, love, and jealousy; chimpanzees are capable of a range of emotions that almost seem human.

Though adults are supposed to be less emotional than children, Hebb is convinced that we become more emotional as we mature. "My theory says that the human adult is more emotional than the three-year-old. Why don't we seem that way? How often have you heard laughter at a funeral? We build human society so that we are carefully protected from our own emotional weaknesses, because we are so easily upset."

SOURCE: Calder, *Mind of Man.*

How Emotional Are You?

How emotional are you? Psychologist Robert Plutchik has charted what he believes are the eight basic emotions. Everyone, except the extremely mentally ill, feels emotions. Some people seem to be firestorms of feeling; others behave like emotional icebergs. Most of us experience a healthy range of emotions balanced between these two extremes. Plutchik shows how the eight basic emotions are experienced by people who are extremely emotional, moderately emotional, and minimally emotional:

Extremely Emotional	Moderately Emotional	Minimally Emotional
Ecstasy	Joy	Pleasure
Adoration	Acceptance	Tolerance
Terror	Fear	Apprehension
Amazement	Surprise	Distraction
Grief	Sadness	Pensiveness
Loathing	Disgust	Boredom
Rage	Anger	Annoyance
Vigilance	Anticipation	Alertness

Only those who fail to experience any of these emotions can be considered mentally ill.

SOURCE: Plutchik, *Emotions*.

Endorphins Have Charms to Soothe the Savage Beast

Do you enjoy the thrill of great music? Ever wonder what makes you feel that way? Is it due to the composer? The musicians? The instruments? The sheer physical sensation of the sound itself? If this were a quiz, and you'd attributed your response to one of the above, you'd have flunked. The correct answer, according to psychopharmacologist Avram Goldstein, is endorphins, natural opiates produced by the brain.

Goldstein arranged for a group of students to listen to their favorite music in a darkened room on headphones. But between sessions, he gave half of the students an endorphin-blocker and the other a placebo. After 19 separate tests, the results were in: Many students who had received the endorphin-blockers failed to experience the sublime thrills from the music felt by their compatriots who received the placebo. Apparently Beethoven and Ice-T just aren't the same without our endorphins.

SOURCE: Avram Goldstein, "Thrills in Response to Music and Other Stimuli," *Physiological Psychology*, Vol. 8, No. 1, 1980.

THINKING

Talking to Yourself

Most of us worry there's something wrong with us when we begin talking out loud to ourselves. But talking to yourself is normal, says research psychologist Eric Klinger. Most people talk to themselves at least once every day. Even when we're not talking out loud, we're still talking to ourselves, mentally. Our inner voice is quiet less than 25 percent of the time. Hearing a snatch of music makes us wonder, What was the name of that song? Thinking about work may trigger the thought, I've got to ask for a raise. Almost everything that happens around us triggers a chain of thoughts, and those thoughts trigger still other thoughts. With this constant mental monologue going on, it's hardly surprising that some "leaks through" from time to time, and we unwittingly find ourselves verbalizing our inner thoughts.

SOURCE: Klinger, *Daydreaming*.

A Penny for Your Thoughts Is Good Pay

"A penny for your thoughts" is a popular saying. If we did get paid a penny for each thought, we'd be earning about $40 each day. Research at the University of Minnesota revealed that we average four separate thoughts per minute—or around 4,000 thoughts a day. It's no wonder our brains feel tired and we are ready to sleep at night.

SOURCE: Ibid.

Superficial Thinkers

When a friend's mind leaps constantly from one subject to another, we call him "scatterbrained" and accuse him of being a "superficial thinker." But new findings about the way our minds work suggest that human beings are a "scatterbrained" species.

While we think a great deal, most of our thoughts are only a few seconds long, according to experiments conducted by psychologist Eric Klinger. Half of our thoughts last 5 seconds or less, most others last less than a minute. Our average "train of thought" occupies a brief 15 seconds. We rarely stick with the same subject for as long as 5 consecutive minutes. Instead, we tend to "think around" a subject, flitting between it and other subjects.

This kind of scatterbrained thinking might seem superficial or even counterproductive. But Klinger believes it actually enriches our thinking. Stray thoughts often lead to solutions for perplexing problems. This kind of "associational" thinking can give the superficial, scatterbrained thinker a distinct advantage over his other more mentally disciplined detractors.

SOURCE: Ibid.

Not Paying Attention

Children are constantly admonished to pay attention. But as adults, few of us seem to be heeding this advice. A recent survey of what people think about on a typical day revealed we concentrate on what we're doing only about a third of the time. Most of our attention is occupied thinking about relationships, personal problems, and people who have made us angry.

Here's what people are actually paying attention to on a typical day:

- **33 percent** concentrating on current surroundings or activities.
- **25 percent** thinking about others and interpersonal relationships.
- **6 percent** active thinking focused on solving problems.
- **3 percent** self-praise or self-criticism.
- **3 percent** anxiety-related thinking.
- **2 percent** self-instruction.

- **1 percent** thinking about violence.
- **26 percent** widely scattered thoughts about a variety of subjects.

SOURCE: Ibid.

Better Brains

Did an insoluble problem or an overwhelming series of events ever make you wish you had a better brain? If so, you probably had in mind all those brilliant, self-composed people who seem to master every challenge and juggle an endless number of activities. Why is life so effortless for them, and so hard for the rest of us?

The answer may be better brains. New research quoted by award-winning science writer Marc McCutcheon, suggests that some people seem to have more efficient neural "wiring." More efficient brain circuitry means they can solve problems more easily and with less effort. No wonder they don't even seem to sweat!

SOURCE: McCutcheon, *Compass in Your Nose.*

COMMUNICATION

Good Listeners

People frequently accuse each other of being poor listeners. But research by R. R. Allen, communications arts professor at the University of Wisconsin, suggests people are better listeners than they realize. If we seem inattentive or bored, it may be because we only manage to get a word in 30 percent of the time—the other 70 percent is spent listening. With that much practice, most of us ought to be good listeners by now.

SOURCE: R. R. Allen, "Communication," *Compton's Encyclopedia.*

Left Speechless

Communication doesn't just involve speech. We can make our meaning clear without ever saying a word. Our body language tells as much, if not more, about our moods and meanings than anything we say.

In a study at England's Birmingham University, psychologist Michael Chance found that gestures can convey meanings as precisely as words. He observed children's arguments and interviewed them afterward. When children lift their hands during an argument, Chance discovered, the position of the hand in relation to the head tells other children exactly how angry or frightened they feel.

SOURCE: Calder, *Mind of Man.*

It Takes Two to Tango

Communication, scientists say, is a two-way street. It requires not only the speaker, but a listener as well. Most of us take our listeners for granted. We have no idea how important they are to us.

Munich researcher Detlev Ploog believes the lone primate is only half a primate. Our interactions with others are not merely tangential to our lives, but critical to them. Apparently, interaction with others releases important brain chemicals, possibly endorphins, that are necessary to our physical and mental health. Unable to communicate with others, we begin to deteriorate. Ploog says that "As a psychiatrist, I believe that the cause of mental illness is a disturbance or even a breakdown of the communication system."

SOURCE: Ibid.

Talked to Death

People who talk too much may be more distracting than most of us realize. Loud, incessant background chatter is a major contributor to lost productivity and impaired performance in the workplace, according to recent Dayton University Psychology Department findings. Their research may also shed light on the source of workplace-related violence.

Test subjects rated random chatter 10 times more distracting than the sound of jackhammers. Subjected to endless doses, they became nervous and irritable, unable to concentrate, and their ability to perform assigned tasks deteriorated. The Dayton researchers concluded that under the right circumstances, prolonged chatter can even drive people to emotional breakdown and violence.

SOURCE: Louis, *1001 Fascinating Facts.*

Oh, Why Do We Lie?

We all tell lies now and then. Most of the lies we tell are white lies, harmless social prevarications related to sparing ourselves and others embarrassment.

When it comes to telling more serious lies, a De Paul University Psychology Department study found we're usually trying to avoid punishment or disapproval. We also lie to make ourselves seem more important and to get our way with others.

SOURCE: "Crosstalk," *Psychology Today*, June 1987.

MEMORY

Moment to Moment

Individuals who suffer serious damage to the brain's hippocampus and amygdala have what scientists call "permanent global anterograde amnesia." These two organs apparently coordinate the processing of our memories. Without them, individuals are unable to store new memories or associate objects with each other. As a result, they live from moment to moment.

SOURCE: Hooper and Teresi, *3-Pound Universe.*

How Many Kinds of Memory Can You Remember?

As if you didn't have enough to remember already, scientists now tell us there are eight kinds of memory, each stored in a different part of the brain.

- **Short-term memory.** Allows us to be aware of what happened recently.
- **Long-term memory.** Allows us to recall events of the past.
- **Verbal memory.** Retains words we've spoken, thought or heard.
- **Spatial memory.** Retains things we've seen and spatial relationships we have experienced.
- **Episodic memory.** Contains our experiences of particular times, places, contexts, and events.
- **Semantic memory.** Contains our knowledge of concepts and language.
- **Procedural memory.** Stores rules, procedures, and "how-to" knowledge.
- **Declarative memory.** Stores facts and other specific items of information.

Now, quick—what kinds of memory were involved in reading this article?

SOURCE: Ibid.

Easy to Remember, and So Hard to Forget

We've all done things we'd rather forget. But we can't, according to brain research pioneer Wilder Penfield. Everything we've ever felt, sensed, done, or experienced is still recorded somewhere within our brains.

Penfield used electricity to stimulate the portions of the brain that store memory. Subjects had sudden flashes from their pasts—

old conversations, cars passing outside a window—complete with all the feelings and sensations of the original event. After seeing small electrical currents miraculously produce many such *tableaux vivants* ("living pictures"), Penfield concluded that our minds store everything that has occurred during our lives. Which may be why some memories keep coming back to haunt us, no matter how hard we try to forget.

SOURCE: Penfield, *Mystery of the Mind*.

Building Your Memory's Muscles

Everyone knows physical exercise causes muscles to swell, but did you know that mental exercise causes your brain to swell? Neuroscientists have found that when a finger is immobilized for a prolonged period, the area of the brain that controls it shrinks. But when the finger is used in a new way, or exercised heavily, that part of the brain actually grows. Muscle builders move over, the beaches may soon be crowded with memory builders.

SOURCE: Campbell, *Musical Brain*.

What Was That Number Again?

If you have trouble remembering seven-digit phone numbers with three-digit area codes, not to mention those nine-digit zip codes, you're not alone. Research shows most of us have a short-term memory capacity of only five to nine digits. This factor was once taken into account when assigning telephone numbers, street addresses, and zip codes. Since then, population growth has swelled cities and nations, causing area codes to proliferate and zip codes to become increasingly complex. Thus, more and more people are going to have more and more difficulty remembering more and more numbers.

SOURCE: Louis, *1001 Fascinating Facts*.

They Remember It Well

Our ability to form new memories peaks in the twenties (not so coincidentally the peak training years of college and our early work experiences). It begins to decline gradually thereafter. By the time we enter our eighties, the brain no longer stores fresh memories as readily.

However, multiple copies of the memories we have already formed are still accessible, stored in many locations throughout the brain. This may explain why older people often recall events of the distant past vividly, but frequently forget trivial short-term data, such as what they ate for breakfast.

SOURCE: McCutcheon, *Compass in Your Nose.*

THE WAY MEMORY WORKS

To Sleep, Perchance to Remember

Researchers have given a new meaning to the phrase "sleep on it." Our retention of new information improves 20 percent to 30 percent if we sleep first, before being tested. Dr. Avi Karni, a neuroscientist at Israel's Weizmann Institute of Science, found that people did better on a test of visual memory after a night's sleep.

In a second series of tests, volunteers in a sleep laboratory were woken up at various times of night. Those who were woken up during the deepest part of sleep, rapid eye movement (REM) sleep, were unable to retain what they had learned the day before. Participants who were not awakened during REM sleep scored higher.

Karni decided there must be an important mechanism in sleep that helps our brains "fix" information learned during the day, especially "how-to" or procedural information. Dr. Karni's advice to those learning a complex, challenging new task—like skiing, a foreign language, or the table of elements—is to "sleep on it."

SOURCE: Sandra Blakeslee, "To Sleep, Perchance to Learn: Neural Links to Memory," *New York Times*, November 3, 1992.

Total Recall

Throughout history there have been people with photographic (eidetic) memories. These remarkable individuals are able to remember everything they see or read. Actor Robert Mitchum was legendary for his ability to memorize a script on a single reading. Writer Isaac Asimov produced more than 300 books during his lifetime, at least in part because whatever he read stuck in his mind.

Most of us have this capacity, but only a few people can access it normally. However, there is evidence that under unusual circumstances—hypnosis, drugs, injury to the brain—anyone can recall past events in minute detail. In London, a woman injured in an auto accident lapsed into a coma and began speaking Greek. A professor of Greek told authorities the woman was reciting the *Iliad* in ancient, not modern, Greek. When she recovered, the woman claimed to have no conscious knowledge of Greek. But she recalled that 30 years earlier she had heard a scholar recite the *Iliad* as she cleaned the building in which he lived.

SOURCE: Louis, *1001 Fascinating Facts.*

That Old Familiar Song

Most parents object when they find their children doing homework while listening to music, concerned that it will interfere with their offspring's ability to retain what they are studying. Now there is evidence that listening to music can actually enhance students' ability to recall their lessons—but only if they listen to the same music when they take the test.

Psychologists at Texas A & M University asked students to study while contemporary music played in the background. Later some students were given tests while the same music played; some were given their tests while different music was played; and some took the tests in silence. The results were conclusive: Students who heard the same music during tests that they heard while studying scored appreciably higher than those who listened to something different or took their tests in silence.

SOURCE: Paul Chance, "Danger: Different Drummer," *Psychology Today*, November 1988.

Why You Can't Find Your Keys

We seem to spend half our time looking for something we've misplaced—lost car keys, missing files, important phone numbers, grandma's recipe for fudge. Often we first search everywhere we normally store the missing item. We then find that we put it away in some far off corner. At the time we were certain we would remember its location, precisely because the spot was so unusual. After all, we reasoned, unusual happenings stand out more vividly in the memory than commonplace ones.

Wrong, says psychologist Eugene Winograd. When it comes to where we put things, we have more trouble remembering the unusual than the usual. In an experiment at Atlanta's Emory University, Winograd found that people consistently recall the location of objects left in usual locations more accurately than those left in unusual spots. A week after the experiment, students were 70 percent less likely to remember where an item was stored if they had not put in a spot where it might normally be found.

SOURCE: Eugene Winograd and Robert Soloway, *Journal of Experimental Psychology*, Vol. 115, No. 4.

If You Can't Trust Your Memory . . .

Most people rely heavily on their memories. I trust my memory, they'll argue, and if their recollection is challenged, they will often offer to bet on it. University of Washington psychologist Elizabeth Loftus says we shouldn't trust our memories, however, and believes memories can become falsified in several ways.

In a series of experiments, Loftus staged fake automobile accidents. She then put eyewitnesses in rooms with fake witnesses who shared fabricated memories of the accident. By the time the real witnesses were called to describe what they'd seen, most had confused the fabricated memories with their own—stop signs became yield signs, barns grew up out of thin air, and yellow cars turned fire-engine red.

We all walk around with false memories, Loftus claims. Our memories become contaminated by our own emotions—we remember it the way we felt it was or wanted it to be—and by the suggestions and recollections of others. Worse, once we have constructed a memory, true or false, we believe it so sincerely that it registers as true on a lie detector.

"There's no way even the most sophisticated hypnotist can tell the difference between a memory that is real and one that's created," Loftus says. "It may be that the legal notion of an independent recollection is a psychological impossibility."

SOURCE: Hooper and Teresi, *3-Pound Universe.*

Memory Cocktails

Having trouble remembering? Swamped by details? Wish you could add more RAM to your brain like you can to your computer? Soon you may be able to do exactly that.

Brain researchers have isolated and duplicated a number of the critical chemicals involved in storing and enhancing memory. Separately, or together, these chemicals point toward the much-heralded "memory pill" we've all been waiting for. These are the chemicals it would contain:

Vasopressin.   Triples the memory span of mice and other mammals.
DDAVP.   Boosts memory in both normal people and victims of Alzheimer's disease (senile dementia).
MSH/ASTH 4-10.   Enhances the attention span and concentration of young and old alike.
Norepinephrine.   Enhances memory and learning.

Enkephalins. Shown to improve learning in rats.

Zimelidine. Restores memory after an alcoholic black out.

'We remember best the things that excite us," psychologist James McGaugh explains. "Arousal causes all these chemical cocktails—norepinephrine, adrenaline, enkephalin, vasopressin, ACTH—to spritz out. . . . These chemicals are memory 'fixatives.' When you are excited or shocked or stressed, they signal the brain, This is important—keep this."

Apparently our memory, like our health, benefits from a good cocktail too.

SOURCE: Ibid.

The Body-Mind Connection

How the Body Affects the Mind

The Body's Messenger Service

We all know the body affects the mind. When we are tired or sick, temper and attention spans shorten, brains turn sluggish, performance declines. When we are healthy and rested, productivity, clear thinking, optimism, and confidence reach a peak.

But how does the condition of the body interact with the mind? Recently scientists discovered the answer. The body's Western Union, says psychobiology researcher Ernest Rossi, Ph.D., is "messenger molecules." Also called "information substances," the body's messenger service employs couriers like: testosterone and estrogen (the sexual hormones); glucose and insulin (which direct energy to various parts of the body); cortisol and adrenalin (which rule awareness and responsiveness); and endorphins and beta-endorphins (which mediate pleasure and relaxation).

"Messenger molecules carry signals about the state of the body's energy level, pain threshold, sex drive, thirst, alertness, pain, pleasure, and mental outlook," Rossi writes. When they reach the brain, these molecules signal us that our body is hungry or full, stressed or relaxed, or needs to be more active or to rest and recuperate. And like most other special delivery messages, we ignore them at our own risk.

SOURCE: Rossi, *Mind-Body Healing.*

Walk It Off

The old advice was right. You can "walk it off." Exercise of any kind releases the same brain chemicals (endorphins) that make us feel happy when we hear good news. When anger, depression, or any other negative emotion has you in its grip, try taking a walk, or engaging in some other physical activity.

Participants in a study by psychology professor Robert E. Thayer were asked to take a 10-minute walk every time they became angry, depressed, or upset over a personal problem. At the end of the walk, the majority reported their negative feelings had dissipated and they felt positive about life again. Evidently when we feel like telling everyone to take a hike, it's time for us to take a walk.

SOURCE: Robert E. Thayer, "Energy Walks," *Psychology Today*, October 1988.

Addicted to Fitness

Exercise is good for us. Its many beneficial effects are drummed into our heads from every side—by fitness gurus, health nuts, even the federal government. But for some women and men, exercise becomes an addiction, as destructive as any other, according to research reported by *Psychology Today*. Joggers who spend all their time at the track, amateur golfers who only live for the game, and weight lifters who constantly haunt the gym may all be flirting with addiction.

The "high" of exercise produced by the endorphins (our body's own homegrown narcotics) traps some. Ironically, the pain attracts others, while still others find exercise a safe place to escape from the real world.

Constant exhaustion, no time for personal relationships, and dangerously overspending on equipment may be signs you've become an exercise junkie.

SOURCE: Eleanor Grant, "The Exercise Fix," *Psychology Today*, February 1988.

The Fantasy or the Erection?

Do women and men get horny because they think about sex? Or do they think about sex because they are horny? Most of the time, the second answer seems to be correct. Some 10 to 15 times each day, our hormones make us begin to think about sex, whether we want to or not.

Every 90 minutes, our bodies release additional testosterone (the hormone governing sexual arousal), according to psychobiology researcher Ernest Rossi. We suddenly find ourselves preoccupied with thoughts of sex. We begin to notice the attractive features of those whose gender arouses us and we may even become partly physically aroused. The effect is even more pronounced in males, who have the highest natural levels of testosterone. It is especially noticeable to their bed partners just after sunrise, when testosterone reaches its daily peak.

SOURCE: Rossi, *Mind-Body Healing*.

Dressing for Distress

Gray flannel suits, dress shirts, and ties have always been part of the male corporate dress for success style. But now there's evidence traditional business attire may be the worst thing success-minded young male executives could wear. Researchers at the textiles and apparel department at Cornell University discovered the constricting pressure of shirt and tie can seriously restrict blood flow to the brain, interfering with men's ability to think clearly, their physical dexterity, and how aware they are of what's happening around them.

The Cornell researchers tested businessmen who habitually

wore suits and ties to work and those who did not. Most participants who wore ties and collars wore them too tight, and this
slowed down their response time in a battery of tests. A second
finding, with strong economic implications for the workplace, was
that even after loosening their collars, participants' response time
was slow to return to normal. This discovery "holds implications
for a variety of other sensory and cognitive functions," the researchers concluded, "including intelligence, creativity, productivity and memory retention." Rather than dressing for success,
these findings suggest most men in gray flannel suits are dressing
for distress.

SOURCE: Leonara M. Langan and Susan M. Watkins, "Human Factors," *Psychology Today*, October 1987.

And Stay Away from Magnets

Eating metals can boost your brain power. Forget your morning
cereal. Instead pass around a heaping bowl of iron and copper,
with a generous sprinkling of zinc for seasoning. You can top off
your tank with up to 20 percent more smarts and acuity for the day
ahead, if you consume your daily share of metals.

Minerals are needed to build neurotransmitters, the brain's
chemical messengers. Iron, zinc, and copper deficiencies dull our
wits. But in one University of Texas study, supplements of these
minerals boosted participants back to normal in just two months.
Those who received zinc or iron supplements improved their
scores an average of 10 percent on tests of memory and cognitive
ability, with some showing improvements of 20 percent and more.

The University of Texas study even revealed which metals we
should take for boosting what parts of our brain. Got a short-term
memory problem? Try iron. Want to improve your ability to associate ideas, objects, and words? Try zinc. For calmness, crunch up
copper. You might want to avoid metal detectors, however.

SOURCE: Bruce Bower, "A Thoughtful Angle on Dreaming," *Science
News*, May 4, 1991; "The Sleep/Mineral Link," *Prevention*, November
1988.

Big, Beefy, and Brain-Damaged

Research shows that natural forms of bodybuilding—exercise, weight lifting, athletics—boost mental health. But steroids and other artificial methods of enhancing musculature may actually cause mental illness. Almost 50 percent of steroid users surveyed in a Mclean Hospital-Harvard Medical School study had experienced serious psychological problems. The results were chilling. Of the bodybuilders surveyed:

33 percent reported major mood swings.
12 percent experienced manic episodes.
12 percent had psychotic episodes.
10 percent manifested "subthreshold psychotic" symptoms.

Steroids increased irritability and aggression in the majority of bodybuilders, and created full-blown delusions in some. One man became convinced jumping from a third-floor window would not hurt him. Another bought two expensive cars he couldn't afford. A third bodybuilder heard nonexistent voices for a period of weeks.

There was one bright light in the Mclean-Harvard report: Most of the symptoms disappeared when users quit taking steroids. They may have been building their bodies, but they were clearly tearing down their minds.

SOURCE: Eleanor Grant, "Of Muscles and Mania," *Psychology Today*, September 1987.

Take Two Before Bedtime

Do you have trouble reaching orgasm? Suffer from depression? Think it's time to see a shrink or a marriage counselor? Before you do, consider this scientific news flash: The problem may not be in your head—it may be in your diet.

Impotence, memory loss, confusion, and depression are just a few of the psychological problems that have been linked to deficiencies in vitamin B_{12} alone. According to Robert Allen, M.D., of the University of Colorado Health Sciences Center in Denver, vitamin B_{12} is as vital to our mental health as it is to our physical health. Many B_{12}-deficient men have solved their erectile problems through vitamin therapy.

SOURCE: "The Sleep/Mineral Link," *Prevention*, November 1988.

The Sweet Smell of Success

Some men and women seem to have gambling on the brain. But for others it may be more in the nose. Tens of thousands of studies have dissected what makes people gamble. Now there's evidence that for some of us, it may be the bouquet of the casino.

Neurologist Alan Hirsch added a pleasant scent to the slot machine area of one Las Vegas casino. Over the next few months, gamblers dropped 45 percent more coins into the machines. Professional ethics prevented Dr. Hirsch from revealing the formula for his fragrance, but for the casino it was clearly "the sweet smell of success."

SOURCE: Beth Ann Krier, "Sweet Smell of Success," *Los Angeles Times*, October 2, 1992.

Peace Pill

The end of war may be in sight, and without unpleasant side effects. Psychopharmacologists in the Netherlands seem to have manufactured an honest-to-goodness antiaggression drug: DU 27716. This miraculous compound dramatically curbed normal interspecies hostility in laboratory rodents. Although male mice normally attack strange mice, males treated with DU 27716 get along fine with strangers and show no traces of anger, aggression, or hostility.

DU 27716 is an antiaggression drug with a plus. Other chemicals that reduce hostility simply sedate people so heavily they are only semiconscious. DU 27716-treated mice are as active and alert

as ever. Better yet, this miraculous chemical erases aggressive violence, but leaves the ability to fight back in self-defense unim-
paired. If subsequent experiments bear out these findings, DU
27716 could be the real post–Cold War "peace dividend."

SOURCE: Hooper and Teresi, *3-Pound Universe.*

What Your Mom Said About Naps Is True

It isn't just children who need to take naps. Adults need naps, too.
Research psychologists at the University of Ottawa report that our
brains function best when we sleep twice a day, not just once.

We all have two major sleep periods, one at night and one in the
afternoon, according to the Ottawa report. The second is much
briefer (usually half an hour to 90 minutes) and arrives about 12
hours after the middle of our previous night's sleep (for most of us,
that's around 3 P.M.). Our brain turns sluggish, our energy reaches
a low, and our body signals its need for a nap with a yawn.

A daily siesta isn't a necessity, the Ottawa researchers found. But
if we didn't get enough sleep the night before, or for several nights
running, obeying the body's urge for a nap becomes critical. We
begin to make mistakes, efficiency declines, we miss important
cues in conversations and work, and we fall asleep on the job. In
short, if you don't take your naps, your body may decide to take
one for you—in the middle of a meeting or a freeway.

SOURCE: Rae Corelli, "The Mysteries of Sleep and Dreams," *Macleans,*
April 23, 1990.

One Hug = 1,000 Words

Children who don't get enough physical affection are at risk of
becoming hard-core felons, rapists, child molesters, and mur-
derers. Monkeys deprived of all physical contact in infancy became aggressive, violent adults, producing the same disturbed EEG
readings as criminally insane patients. Research by James Prescott
of the National Institute of Child Health and Human Develop-

ment showed both groups shared a serious disorder of the limbic pain-pleasure system.

Sensory stimulation plays a vital role in the growth of infants' brain structures, especially the all-powerful limbic system. The biological systems that signal pleasure don't develop normally in children who receive little or no hugging, touching, or contact. All they can experience is pain, and when that happens they may develop into violent adults.

If his findings were correct, Prescott reasoned, "cultures that give infants a lot of physical affection—touching, holding, and carrying—would be less physically violent, and they are." He surveyed 49 cultures, from the peace-loving Maoris to the martial Comanche, in the United States, Italy, France, Japan, Australia, Mexico, and South America. Prescott's theory held true: Crime, violence, and child abuse (along with such customs as killing, torturing, or mutilating the enemy) were rare or unknown in cultures where parents were nourishing and physically affectionate.

Prescott's researchers may even provide the key to a winning strategy in the war on crime—and one that won't cost taxpayers an additional cent. "I'm now convinced," he says, "that the root cause of violence is deprivation of physical pleasure. When you stimulate the neurosystems that mediate pleasure, you inhibit the systems that mediate violence."

SOURCE: Hooper and Teresi, *3-Pound Universe*.

Suicidal Brains

Prescott's discoveries may tie into experiments on the brains of suicide victims at Israel's Weizmann Institute of Science. People often try to take their own lives because the brain's "pain switches" get stuck at "on," while their "pleasure switches" are stuck at "off." The institute's Ruth Gross-Isserof probed the innermost recesses of the brain cells of women and men who had died by their own hands. She found they shared characteristic irregularities of the opioid receptors, which play critical roles in sensations of well-being and suffering.

People often kill themselves following a long-term depression.

"The essence of depression is anhedonia, an inability to experience pleasure," explains Anat Biegon, who co-chaired the Weizmann project from the New York University School of Medicine. "And opioid receptors are the primary targets of the brain's reward system."

Men and women born with disorders of the opioid system may have brains "wired" for suicide. If so, Gross-Isserof and Biegon's discoveries offer more reason for rejoicing than for despair. If proven, their work may point the way toward a chemical cure for those "suicidal brains."

SOURCE: Bruce Bower, "Suicide Brains: Naturally Prone to Pain?" *Science News*, November 10, 1990.

The Scent of Serenity

It may not be music, but scent that soothes the savage beast. Scientists at Yale University discovered some fragrances have a calming effect; they can even lower blood pressure. Researchers there devised an apple-spice fragrance that stopped panic attacks. The university plans to patent the formula and license it for commercial use.

As most aficionados of the shore know, the aroma of the ocean can also be very relaxing. In one study at England's University of Warwick, uptight, agitated men and women were exposed to a "beach perfume" containing essence of seaweed. Anxiety levels decreased as much as 18 percent after subjects had whiffed the tangy scent of the sea.

SOURCE: McCutcheon, *Compass in Your Nose*.

Some Are Born with It

Does our body chemistry dictate our personality? Or does our personality dictate our body chemistry? Aggressive, dominant men—type A personalities who become leaders and authority figures—have long been known to have twice the normal level of serotonin in their blood. Psychiatrist Michael McGuire wanted to know if leaders are simply born with more serotonin, or do their serotonin levels rise with their social rank?

In a study of monkeys, McGuire removed type A leaders from the group and isolated them in solitary cages for a few weeks. Sure enough, with no one to boss around and boost their egos, the levels of serotonin in the leaders' blood promptly halved. But when McGuire restored the type A's to their group, they quickly displaced the new leaders who had taken over in their absence, and their serotonin level returned to normal.

The evidence seemed to suggest personality ruled body chemistry. But McGuire decided to confirm his results by reversing the experiment. He boosted serotonin levels in passive monkeys and saw timid, insecure males swagger and grow authoritative.

McGuire concluded there was a symbiotic relationship. Our bodies and minds interact to determine what we are and how we feel, and which has the greatest influence changes according to what's going on in and around us. McGuire's work seems to suggest that some are born as type A's; some become type A's; and some have type A personalities thrust upon them.

SOURCE: Hooper and Teresi, *3-Pound Universe*.

Riding the Waves

The term *body surfing* may soon take on a whole new meaning. Waves of alertness wash through our minds in 90-minute cycles (ultradian cycles) triggered by messenger molecules from the body's limbic and endocrine systems. For an hour and 15 minutes out of every hour and half, the body sends signals (via adrenaline, noradrenaline, and other alertness drugs) that keep our minds at a peak of awareness, energy, physical skills, memory, learning ability, and productivity. Then, for the next 15 to 20 minutes, the body sends our minds into a low, as it secretes chemicals that repair the stress and strains created by these alertness messengers, while recharging our batteries for renewed endeavors.

Midway through the active part of this cycle, we are at our most efficient, mentally and physically, according to Ernest Rossi, Ph.D., psychobiology researcher. Verbal and spatial skills, eye-hand coordination, memory, alertness, creativity, and productivity reach a crest. We feel energized, in tune with the universe, and seem able to cope with most problems effortlessly.

Midway through the downswing of this cycle, our awareness of the outer world declines to a minimum (as alertness chemicals fall), while the barriers to our inner world fall away. Mind and body are in the ideal state for tapping intuition, mental rehearsal, and emotional and physical healing and seeking creative inspiration. We feel sleepy, sluggish, daydreamlike, and become introspective.

Rossi claims that those who learn to ride the "waves" of the body's 90-minute ultradian cycle can:

- Match critical work with periods of maximum productivity.
- Maintain personal energy throughout the day.
- Break patterns of stress and tension.
- Reap the maximum benefit from moments of greatest insight and creativity.
- Enhance physical and mental well-being.

SOURCE: Rossi, *20-Minute Break*.

It's a Wise Mom

Mothers and their babies seem to be able to identify each other instinctively. Advocates of parapsychology claim it's ESP. But a series of studies cited in *Psychology Today* suggest a more mundane solution: It may be the nose that knows.

Psychologist Michael Russell found 6 out of 10 babies could identify the scent of their mother's breast pads. Moms were just as quick to sniff out their own newborns. The same percentage of mothers could identify their babies by scent only hours after birth. Mothers were equally adept at sniffing out clothing worn by their older children.

SOURCE: Paul McCarthy, "Scent: The Tie That Binds?" *Psychology Today*, July 1986.

HOW THE MIND AFFECTS THE BODY

Gut Feelings

Having a gut feeling may be more than just a figure of speech. The communication system between mind and body is a two-way street. Our brain, nervous system, immune system, and endocrine system are so closely linked that they constitute a single master network, says Candace Pert, chief of brain biochemistry at the National Institute of Mental Health.

The mind communicates with the body via the same messenger molecules the body uses to signal the brain. Among these are neuropeptides (endorphins, vasopressin, factor S, bombesin) that regulate our moods and emotions. The body doesn't just flood the brain with peptides; our bloodstream carries them to muscles, heart, lungs, liver, intestines, and other organs as well. Clear proof, Pert says, "emotions are not just [experienced] in the brain, they're in the body."

Like and dislike send neuropeptides flooding through our bodies, and we experience these as gut reactions.

SOURCE: Rossi, *Mind-Body Healing*; Justice, *Who Gets Sick*.

It's All in Your Head

Forget germs, microbes, bacteria, viruses, and all the other causes of illness you learned about in school. New scientific understanding of why we get sick says it's our mental health that rules our physical health, writes Blair Justice, Ph.D. Most of the "bugs" that cause illness already reside in our bodies. Our thoughts, beliefs, attitudes, and emotional stance, not our bodies, make the difference between coming down with an infection or staying in good health.

How resistant we are to disease depends on our characteristic way of responding to the difficulties and challenges of life, and the chemical changes those responses cause. Our moods and feelings register in our brain's hypothalamus, which signals our endocrine and nervous systems to trigger the release of pleasure-pain hormones (especially neuropeptides and adrenaline). These in turn determine the health and well-being of key elements of our immune system: white blood cells, T cells, and macrophages (scavenger cells that aid in our defense against disease).

When our responses to problems in life are negative (fearful, angry, despairing) the hormones our brains release weaken the body's defenses. Our body's indigent microbes and viruses run wild, and we become prey to illness from within and without. When our responses are positive (optimistic, loving, humorous) the hormones our brains release strengthen our immune system.

SOURCE: Ibid.

What Makes Us Well

Throw away those expensive pills and cigarettes. Dump all the booze down the sink. Cancel those expensive therapy sessions. Your mind and body have their own built-in antidotes for stress. Scientists call it the relaxation response. When we are completely relaxed, our bloodstream becomes flooded with chemicals that counteract the harmful effects of stress and promote optimal health. These chemicals include endorphins, benzodiazepines, and other neuropeptides—the same hormones released when we are happy, optimistic, or laughing.

The term *relaxation response* was coined by cardiologist Herbert Benson, director of the Hypertension Section of Beth Israel Hospital in Boston. Benson studied the psychological and physical conditions involved in deep relaxation. A restful environment, mental silence, a comfortable posture, and slow, even breathing were always involved. Benson wondered if people could learn to consciously induce the relaxation response to counter stress and its effects.

He placed volunteers in quiet, comfortable rooms and worked with them to duplicate the quiet mind and measured breathing of the relaxation response. Millions have since used this technique, or one of its many variations, to reverse the damage of stress. What Benson had discovered was a technique handed down from beyond the dawn of history, through the world's oldest religions and philosophies, variously named "meditation," "prayer," and "yoga."

SOURCE: Harman and Rheingold, *Higher Creativity*; Justice, *Who Gets Sick*.

Stressing Out

Stress is probably the best-known effect of attitude and mood on physical health. Newspapers, magazines, and radio and television programs have all popularized stress as our number one health concern. Stress has surpassed the common cold as the most prevalent health problem in America, according to Paul Rosch, M.D., head of the American Institute of Stress.

Stress-related conditions cost the United States $10 billion to $20 billion annually in lost productivity. And they have been indicted as a leading killer of men and women. Even a brief list of the psychological and physical problems stress causes reads like a who's who of modern illnesses:

Physical effects. Hypertension, heart disease, strokes, aneurysms, ulcers, cancer, impotence, frigidity, decreased fertility, migraines, backaches, asthma, bronchitis, digestive disorders, skin problems, sleep disorders.

Emotional effects. Depression, bulimia, anorexia, anxiety, crying spells, paranoia, addiction, chronic anger, suicide, domestic violence, panic.

Unfortunately, many stress-prone men and women tend to worry about the effects of stress on their life. For them, mental life becomes a vicious circle as they stress out about stress.

SOURCE: Justice, *Who Gets Sick*.

Stress: It May Not Be Bad for You

Now, ignore everything you've heard about stress. It may not be the villain it's been painted. Psychologists Suzanne Kobasa and Salvatore Maddi decided to test the popular theory that high stress means increased risk of illness. Kobasa and Maddi surveyed 200 managers and executives who had recently experienced severe stress. Half had suffered stress-related illnesses, but half were as healthy as any other group.

Clearly, heightened stress didn't make everyone ill. Women and men who stayed healthy, the researchers discovered, had a different way of looking at and dealing with stressful events than those who became sick. Healthy executives shared a relaxed attitude toward problems. They:

- Embraced change, good or bad, as an inevitable part of life and an opportunity for growth, and not as a threat to their security.
- Never viewed setbacks and disasters as the end of the world or beyond repair.
- Were confident they could control the impact of problems when they occurred.
- Were deeply involved with families, work, and friends.
- Possessed a strong sense of commitment, meaning, and direction in their lives.
- Believed in the importance and value of who they were and what they were doing.

Kobasa and Maddi's discoveries suggest it's not the stress in our lives, but how lively we are when stressed, that counts.

SOURCE: Justice, *Who Gets Sick.*

MIND OVER MATTER

Caution—Humor May Be Hazardous to Your Illness

A laugh a day may do more to keep the doctor away than an apple, according to psychiatrist William Frey. Laughter may not be the best medicine, but there's solid evidence a sense of humor may be one of the most potent medicines in the modern physician's pharmacopoeia. Researchers at dozens of hospitals and medical centers have established beyond doubt that laughing at life's problems strengthens our ability to resist disease, fight infection, and recover from injury or surgery.

Psychiatrist William Frey claims laughing produces the same physical effects as exercise. Twenty seconds of laughter puts our cardiovascular, muscular, and respiratory systems through a workout equal to 20 minutes of aerobics. Laughter also reduces stress and stress-related diseases like high blood pressure, heart disease, and stroke. In one famous experiment, Harvard psychologist David McClelland found infection-fighting proteins in the bloodstream increased after participants viewed comedy films.

Among mirth's many benefits, it:

- Releases anger, depression, and other negative emotions.
- Helps us transcend worry and tension.
- Uplifts, encourages, and empowers.
- Draws our attention away from our troubles.
- Puts problems in perspective.
- Keeps us balanced.

Without laughter, we'd be sick far more often than we are, Frey concludes. Humor, it appears, is no laughing matter.

SOURCE: Frey and Salameh, *Handbook of Humor*; Klein, *Healing Power of Humor*.

It Only Hurts When I Don't Laugh

Laughter may not only be your best medicine, it may be your best anesthetic, too. Rosemary Cogan, Ph.D., a Texas Tech psychologist, decided to test the effects of laughter on our ability to withstand pain. Using mild electroshocks, participants' pain thresholds were measured before and after they listened to a comedy tape. Students who laughed out loud withstood 20 percent more pain than other students. Subsequent research found laughter releases opiates like the endorphins, the body's own natural painkillers. The old movie cliché of the hero who laughs at wounds because he feels no pain may be true—only he may not be feeling any pain because he's laughing at his wounds.

SOURCE: Rosemary Cogan, *Journal of Behavioral Medicine*, Vol. 10, 1987.

Health: It's Who You Know

Everybody needs a sense of connection, whether to a person or a group. Now there's evidence lovers and friends are not only good for your psyche, they may be good for your health as well. Women and men who reported a strong sense of connection to others showed greater resistance to disease, revealed one U.S. Department of Health, Education, and Welfare survey.

There is mounting evidence that "organic diseases are linked to ... the nature of one's relationships with others and to one's position in the social world," according to Robert Ornstein, Ph.D., and David Sobel, M. D. The more we accept our need for others, it seems, the less we need physicians. When it comes to health, as in business and politics, it's who we know that counts.

SOURCE: Robert Ornstein and David Sobel, "The Healing Brain," *Psychology Today*, March 1987.

One Person's Pain

Pain isn't all in your head, but how *much* it hurts may be. Fear of suffering can actually increase the amount of pain an injury causes. Combat vets wounded in battle require only a fraction the pain-killer civilian surgical patients require, according to a study by H.K. Beecer.

Wounded soldiers interpret the pain of their wounds as an end to the horror and stress of combat, Beecer theorizes, while civilian patients view the pain of surgery as part of an unpleasant experience associated with helplessness, disease, and death. One person's pain *can* be the end of another's suffering.

SOURCE: Fishman, *Bomb in the Brain.*

Medicine: Half of It May Be in Your Mind

There's good evidence we only get half the benefit from our pills and medicines we think we do. Half or more of the money we spend on medication is probably wasted. That's what scientists discovered when they conducted research into the "placebo effect."

Placebos are "dummy" pills that contain no medicine. When pharmaceutical companies test new medications, half the participants are unknowingly given placebos; the other half receive the actual drug. Supposedly if a medicine proves effective, the half that received the real drug would improve, while those who received the placebo would not.

But researchers have found that at least 50 percent of those given placebos get well, too. Because participants believed they had been given medicine that would make them better, those beliefs proved as powerful as any medicine scientists tested. In studies reported in *The American Journal of Psychiatry*, placebos were effective on an awesome variety of complaints: angina, warts, asthma, pain, arthritis, anger, insomnia, obesity, nightmares, anxiety, mood swings, addiction, impotence, and frigidity.

Could the placebo effect help slow down the spiraling costs of drugs? It's possible. The power of belief may have unlimited healing power.

SOURCE: Justice, *Who Gets Sick*; Smith, *Powers of the Mind.*

On the Blink

Remember mood rings? Their colors changed with the wearer's feelings. Other people could tell our moods just by looking at the ring. Now science has discovered an even surer gauge of our feelings: the frequency of our blinking.

Most adults blink about 15 times per minute. However, according to experiments cited in *Psychology Today*, our emotional states affect blinking: We blink faster when angry, frightened, or lying; drug use causes us to blink more slowly; tiredness makes blinks last longer. Trained observers are thus able to read our mood in the blink of an eye.

SOURCE: Susan Chollar, "In the Blink of an Eye," *Psychology Today*, March 1988.

No Wonder It Drives Rock Fans Wild

For years critics have claimed rock music was an insidious influence that drove youth crazy, or worse. Now a Connecticut hospital study suggests there may be more fire than smoke in these claims. Psychiatric patients who watched a rock music video channel developed hallucinations, increased belligerence, and greater hostility toward the staff. Once music videos were banned, the effects rapidly wore off. Considering the much headlined idiosyncrasies of rock stars—listeners may not be the only ones affected.

SOURCE: "News of . . . ," *Los Angeles Reader*, October 12, 1992.

Not Tonight Honey, I've Got a Muscle Ache

People who have headaches from stress and overwork often say, My brain hurts. But they're wrong. The brain actually has no pain receptors and can't feel pain. The "ache" in the headache comes from contractions or dilations in muscles and blood vessels outside the brain, usually caused by stress, anger, or disappointment. It may feel like the pain's inside our heads, but it's actually outside, in the scalp, sinuses, blood vessels, and muscles of the face, head, eye, or neck.

SOURCE: Columbia University, *Complete Home Medical Guide.*

Getting High on Help

There's a new legal high on the horizon. It's clean. Its free. And it has positive side effects. Helping others gets you high, according to an Institute for the Advancement of Health analysis. More than 1,700 volunteers reported helping others produced the same sense of well-being as exercise and meditation. Doing good unto others really does result in doing good unto yourself.

SOURCE: Alan Lulks, "Helper's High," *Psychology Today*, October 1988.

The Incredible Shrinking You

How tall are you? It may be time to haul out the measuring tape. You may not be the height you remember. Or the height you were yesterday, or even 10 minutes ago. We grow taller or shorter with our mood, according to research reported in *Woman's Day*.

Happiness can subtract as much as half an inch from our height; our bodies actually shrink as muscle tension eases. Stress can add half an inch, as muscle tension draws us inward and upward. So can the unconscious inner tensing scientists say many of us experience when we are publicly pointed out for exceptional achievement (popularly known as "drawing oneself up with pride"). No wonder we speak of pride making us feel 10 feet tall.

SOURCE: Judith Chase Churchill, "That's Life," *Woman's Day*, May 1992.

Our Conscious and Unconscious Selves

The Iceberg's Tip

One Giant Step for Humankind

What's the most important advance in the history of humankind? Fire? The wheel? Religion? The microchip?

The answer may lie further back—some 500,000 years, in fact, according to *The Encyclopaedia of Ignorance*. Nobel laureate neuroscientist Roger Sperry believes it is the evolutionary debut of consciousness. Sperry calls it "the most critical step in the whole of evolution."

SOURCE: Roger Sperry, "Problems Outstanding in the Evolution of Brain Function," Duncan and Weston-Smith, eds., *The Encyclopaedia of Ignorance*.

A 10 Percent Tip

Your consciousness seems all-encompassing. Sitting here, reading this book, you are aware of the words on the page, the page itself, the book, the chair you sit in, your body, the room around you, many of its contents, and all the sights, sounds, and scents that fill it. You're also aware of the meaning of the words you read, your own responses to them, the host of associated thoughts and feelings they stir up, and even strong memories of the events of the day so far and anticipations of events to come.

What could be more complete? Yet researchers at Stanford Research Institute say consciousness represents only the tip of our mental iceberg—a mere 10 percent—the smallest sliver of the vast mechanism that makes up our minds.

SOURCE: Harman and Rheingold, *Higher Creativity.*

Don't Give It a Second Thought

Most of us never give consciousness a second thought. We are rarely conscious of the fact that we are conscious. Just keeping abreast of all the things we are conscious of—our problems, our lives, the unfolding events of the world around us—overloads our mental resources. Nature may have planned it that way.

Research by psychiatrist Howard Shevrin at the University of Michigan Medical Center suggests the mind has mechanisms designed to minimize those moments when we become aware of being conscious. Other research has shown that thinking about what we're thinking can interfere with our original train of thought. Still others have demonstrated that self-consciousness interferes with performance and that we tend to be more morbid, insecure, and worried about our mental health when we are aware of and thinking about our minds and consciousness.

When it comes to most things in life, it's usually wisest to think them through two or three times. But when it comes to consciousness, its apparently wisest not to give it a second thought.

SOURCE: Laurence Miller, "In Search of the Unconscious," *Psychology Today,* December 1986.

All the Mind's a Stage

Consciousness is our awareness of what goes on in and around us and of the link between these incidents and ourselves as the one who experiences them. It's what makes the "self" possible. "Those things of which we are conscious, and the ways in which we are conscious of them, determine what it is like to be us," according to Douglas Hofstadter and Daniel Dennett.

Psychologist John F. Kihlstrom of the University of Arizona calls consciousness the staging area of the mind. It holds together the moments just past, the present moment, and those coming into existence, knitting them together with everything we have been and everything we are now—while being aware in individually worded thoughts of all that comes to our attention. It is this staging area that creates our sense of ourselves as an integrated personality moving through time.

SOURCE: Hofstadter and Dennett, *Mind's I*; John Kihlstrom, "The Cognitive Unconscious," *Science*, September 18, 1987.

Center of Consciousness

Where is our consciousness located? We know it's somewhere inside our head, because that's where our thought and awareness take place. If you wanted to find it, according to current research, you would have to descend between the lobes of the brain, past the ridged girdle of the cingulate gyrus, through the hard body of the corpus callosum into a twisting, bottlelike labyrinth. You have reached the interlocked organs of the reticular activating and limbic systems: the thalamus, the hypothalamus, the hippocampus, the pineal gland, the amygdala, and the caudate nucleus. Though all parts of the brain work together in creating consciousness, mental activity depends on the normal functioning of this area of the brain.

SOURCE: Rossi, *Mind-Body Healing*.

You're Not Alone in the Voting Booth

Does your view of consciousness determine how you vote? Neurobiologist Roger Sperry thinks it does. Most of us don't quickly perceive the link between consciousness and such elephantine institutions as the courts, the welfare system, religion, the military, and multinational corporations. But according to Sperry, there is a connection. "Social values depend . . . on whether consciousness is believed to be mortal, immortal, reincarnate, or cosmic . . . localized and brain-bound or essentially universal." Sperry might have added: To what degree we believe consciousness is dictated by chemical and electrical interactions and whether free will exists (and if so to what extent, considering what we know of the influence of hormones, family environment, and even genetics). Our view of consciousness determines so much of what we think about social and moral values because it's nothing less than our view of what we think it means to be us—and to be human. We take this view with us everywhere we go, from the voting booth to church, the bedroom, the boardroom, and all the other aspects of our lives.

SOURCE: Harman and Rheingold, *Higher Creativity*.

Double Vision

Have you ever had a memory so vivid it seemed as if you were back at that moment in the past? Most people have. Scientists call such experiences "dual consciousness."

In the laboratory, when electrodes stimulate the parts of the brain responsible for memory, past experiences are suddenly replayed with their original intensity and vividness. In daily life, electrical impulses generated by the brain itself set off "dual consciousness" and its flood of vivid memories. For those who have this unique experience, the stream of consciousness is suddenly doubled, according to Wilder Penfield, Ph.D., the dean of brain researchers.

Those who experience dual consciousness do not confuse the vision with reality, according to Penfield. Subjects are aware of what is going on around them as well as the "flashback" from the past.

Surely there's a fortune to be made by the first scientist who can show dieters how to produce dual consciousness at will, enabling them to savor flavorsome feasts from the past while munching down a tasteless low-cal preparation.

SOURCE: Penfield, *Mystery of the Mind*.

Teamwork

It not only takes two to tango—it takes two to create consciousness (two neurons that is). Wolf Singer at Germany's famed Max
Planck Institute for Brain Research seems to have proven that at
least two brain cells (one in each hemisphere) must fire for us to
become conscious of a stimulus, such as the color red or the
touch of a feather. Studying the way cats' brains work, Singer
found that neurons at widely separated locations fire syn-
chronous electrical impulses when the brain responds to stimuli
from an object.

Other neuroscientists believe Singer has discovered the "philosopher's stone" of all brain research: the cellular basis of consciousness. Singer's experiments seem to answer the fundamental
question of how neurons at different locations can pool their
information to create a coherent image and how the brain might
link these with the cells responsible for ideas and thoughts. They
may do it, Singer suggests, simply by firing in unison.

Like so much else in life, consciousness seems to require team-
work.

SOURCE: Marcia Barinaga, "The Mind Revealed," *Science*, August 24,
1990.

Why We All Can't See Eye to Eye

Most of us assume that there is one "normal" state of consciousness and that it is pretty much the same for everybody. But that's
not true, according to Candace Pert, Ph.D., a researcher at the
National Institute of Mental Health. Just as there are enormous
variations among humans in height, intelligence, and skill, there
are also enormous variations in brain components and chemistry,
two factors that affect 90 percent or more of our state of consciousness. At one extreme are those of us who always see the
positive in life; at the other end are those who only see the
negative. Some people relate to words best, others to visual cues.

Some are very intuitive, while others see everything in logical terms.

Rather than there being a single, common state of consciousness shared by all, there is a "spectrum composed of discrete states of consciousness," writes psychologist Jon Klimo, Ph.D. These states of consciousness include: daydreaming, hypnotic trances, out-of-body experiences, peak performance states, moments of intense insights, religious ecstasy, meditative contemplation, prolonged sleeplessness, and dozens, perhaps hundreds, of others. Moreover, Pert claims, "We don't all start from the same baseline of consciousness, and we vary widely in our ability to transit between different states. What one person experiences as an altered state may fall into the sphere of ordinary consciousness for another."

SOURCE: Klimo, *Channeling*; Hooper and Teresi, *3-Pound Universe*.

ALTERED STATES

As American as Apple Pie

Have you experienced an altered state of consciousness (ASC) recently? Most of us answer no (unless we're drug users or meditators). But we're mistaken, claims Charles Tart, Ph.D., University of California at Davis psychologist and coiner of the term "altered states of consciousness." Our consciousness fluctuates constantly in response to what we eat, breathe, feel, and think.

Suddenly, without warning, we find ourselves in a different state of consciousness. We might catch ourselves drifting off into vivid daydreams; in a state of heightened awareness; pulling into our parking space with no memory of driving there; or feeling unaccountably depressed.

Scientists have catalogued a multitude of altered states of consciousness. Among them are: reveries, daydreaming, hypnosis, out-of-body experiences, peak experiences, channeling, mystical trances, religious ecstasy, fuzzy-mindedness, meditation, near death experiences, creative inspiration, the auras we see during migraines, sleepiness, drunkenness, uncontrollable rage, and inner peace. ASCs are produced in an equally fascinating variety of ways: through exercise, fasting, prayer, dance, sleeplessness, fever, chanting, hypnosis and self-hypnosis, hyperventilation, hypoglycemia, biofeedback, and of course drugs and chemicals.

ASCs may seem strange, unreal, even threatening—but they're really "as all-American as apple pie and the Superbowl," according to Tart. In fact, almost all the world's cultures have institutionalized mind-altering rituals, says anthropologist Erica Bourguignon. Amazonian Indians have tribal ceremonies that create ASCs and we have ours: cocktail parties, dance clubs with strobe lights, television, and evangelical religion. "The fact that they are nearly universal," Bourguignon tells us, "must mean that such states are very important to human beings."

For one thing, they sure help break the monotony.

SOURCE: Hooper and Teresi, 3-Pound Universe.

A Little Silence, Please

What's older than the dawn of history, and as modern as today's neuroscientific research? Need a hint? It's been shown to cure mental and physical illness and provide solutions to your most pressing problems. Give up? It's meditation.

Meditation quiets our usually busy consciousness. By stilling the mind, we achieve heightened mental clarity. According to physician-researcher Harold Bloomfield, multiple experiments prove meditation produces positive feelings that promote emotional health and add noticeably to self-esteem and sociability. It also reduces anxiety, tension, irritability, chronic fatigue, and depression, while doubts and insecurities fade.

The mental quiet and relaxation produced by meditation confers profound benefits on the body as well as the mind. "Inner silence is crucial to health," Bloomfield claims. "One experiences a state of deep rest, marked by decreases in heartbeat rate, oxygen consumption, perspiration, muscle tension, blood pressure and levels of stress hormones."

No wonder meditation is still around after hundreds of thousands of years.

SOURCE: Bloomfield, "Healing Silence"; Justice, *Who Gets Sick.*

You Can't Just Sit There and Do Nothing

Meditation may seem mysterious and difficult. But it's really as easy as falling off a log, says Herbert Benson, M.D. Benson has successfully taught thousands to meditate in the laboratory. It may take a few tries to get the hang of meditation, but he promises that you'll soon notice its physical and mental benefits.

Benson's research shows that four things are necessary to produce a state of deep meditation: (1) a quiet environment to eliminate distractions; (2) a comfortable posture that allows complete relaxation; (3) a few moments spent relaxing; and (4) a mental device (traditionally called a mantra or prayer) to help block the endless flow of thoughts generated by our waking mind.

To meditate, begin by slowly relaxing all your muscles, Benson advises, starting at your feet and ending with your neck, head, and face. Then for the next 10 to 20 minutes, while keeping the muscles relaxed, breathe in and out easily and naturally, mentally saying *one* (or the mental device of your choice) with each in-breath.

Why meditation? Why not just sit quietly and relax? Because simple relaxation doesn't produce the same mental and physical benefits as meditation. One joint Oxford University and University of London research project found meditation programs are far more effective at reducing stress than just relaxing.

SOURCE: Benson, *Relaxation Response*; Clive Wood, "Relaxation Really Works," *Psychology Today*, January 1987.

You're the One

It's the most sublime of all mental experiences: A sudden, almost mystical sense of oneness and harmony with the universe. Those who've had it report a profound sense of awe, wonder, and overflowing love for everything around them. Psychologist Abraham Maslow called it "unitive consciousness."

Such experiences were once thought the province of mystics and the highly religious. But scientists like Spencer Sherman, Ph.D., have taught others to induce unitive experiences in the laboratory through biofeedback, meditation, and self-hypnosis. Volunteers recounted the same feelings of oneness with everything, the same sense of peace and awe.

More significantly, personality profiles and detailed interviews with family, friends, and colleagues suggest laboratory-induced mystical experiences create the same dramatic and lasting personality changes produced by years of psychotherapy. "These include," writes psychologist Roger Walsh, Ph.D., "an increased belief in afterlife; a greater sense of the preciousness of relationships, love, and life; more interest in learning and self knowledge; and a significant shift from materialistic goals and possessions toward helping and caring for others."

SOURCE: Ring, *Heading Toward Omega*; Walsh, *Spirit of Shamanism*.

Out of It

Have you ever suddenly found yourself floating outside your body—free to move around from room to room, even to distant locations? If so, you're in good company. A full third of us report having an "out of body experience" (OBE), according to a survey conducted by Britain's Institute of Psychophysical Research and Australia's University of New England.

How real are OBEs? Skeptics dismiss them as hallucinations, daydreams, and microdreams. But Stanford Research Institute (SRI) experiments in "remote viewing" suggest we may actually possess the ability to travel mentally while leaving our bodies behind. In one test, women and men were given a randomly chosen latitude and longitude, then asked to visualize sending their minds out to that location. Similarities between sketches they made of what they "saw" and photographs taken at the location were astonishingly high.

"If the SRI results are accurate, the ability to know what is happening at a place one has never visited is not a rare talent," Willis Harman, President of the Institute for the Noetic Sciences wrote. Instead, it lies latent within all of us. The Stanford researchers even developed a program that enabled participants to learn remote viewing. Traveling mentally, they concluded, is a trainable skill anyone can learn.

SOURCE: Talbot, *Holographic Universe*; LaBerge, *Lucid Dreaming*.

So Near and Yet So Far

Your heart has stopped—by all medical standards, you are clinically dead. Yet you don't feel dead. Instead, you find yourself outside your lifeless body, moving down a dark tunnel. A profound sense of peace and well-being fills you. You know you are dead, but you feel no fear, for you now know there is life beyond death. An incomprehensibly brilliant light radiates from the tunnel's end. As you enter the light, deceased friends and loved ones greet you in an atmosphere of love, peace, and joy. They help you review your life, then persuade you to re-enter the body to complete unfinished business in the world of the living.

Abruptly you find yourself back in your body. Doctors state you were clinically dead—pulse, heart, and brainwaves stopped—then revived by the miracles of medical science. Like most men and women who have died and been resuscitated, you have just had a near death experience (NDE). Many scoff at these accounts, passing them off as hallucinations or wish-fulfilling dreams. But surveys reported by psychiatrist Roger Walsh, Ph.D., reveal those who've had NDEs dumbfounded doctors with detailed descriptions of what occurred in the operating room while they were pronounced clinically dead.

Women and men who have undergone NDEs report them as major turning points in their lives. Research backs up these accounts of dramatic psychological growth, Walsh writes. That may explain why 9 out of 10 people would be willing to have an NDE again. For all the attraction of near death experiences, however, the stiff admission requirements ensure they won't become a fad anytime soon.

SOURCE: Walsh, *Spirit of Shamanism*; Ring, *Heading Toward Omega*.

Mind Spas

Peace of mind and spiritual bliss used to be counted among the things money can't buy. But no more. Today, you can rent them by the hour.

Mind spas, as this growing new business is called, are springing up in most big cities. Satori, bliss, and perfect relaxation are served up to order. Job and memory performance boosts are house specialties.

Just slip off your shoes, put on the special goggles and headphones, and your friendly neighborhood mind spa does the rest. A combination of spinning colors and pulsing tones send you drifting in and out of meditationlike states. Bizarre as it seems, this high-tech route to altered states of consciousness has a solid scientific basis.

Researchers at St. Luke Medical Center discovered that exposure to patterns of audio and visual pulses causes the brain to change states of consciousness. With one pattern, they induced the deep relaxation associated with theta waves, easing chronic pain and increasing alertness. With another pattern they induced the alert attention associated with beta waves, helping women and men improve motivation and break the chains of addiction. Forget mental discipline and spiritual attainment—enlightenment and out-of-body experiences have just joined the list of things money *can* buy.

SOURCE: Linda Williams with Selichi Kanise, "Turn On and Tune Out," *Time*, February 26, 1990.

THE OTHER 90 PERCENT

Subconscious or Unconscious?

Subconscious, unconscious—everyone gets them mixed up. Haven't we heard that 90 percent of the mind's processes take place beneath the surface in the subconscious? And aren't we all motivated by forces from somewhere deep in our subconscious minds?

Well, no. Psychiatrist Jerrold Maxmen, Ph.D., says you can tell those who lack psychiatric sophistication because they say *subconscious* instead of *unconscious*. Freud popularized the term *subconscious* in his pioneer 1893 tome *Studies on Hysteria*, only to outlaw its use 20 years later and replace it with *unconscious*. Today, Maxmen writes, psychiatrists never use the term *subconscious*—they always say *unconscious*.

SOURCE: Maxmen, *New Psychiatry*.

Not a Swelled Head

It's not surprising that 90 percent of our mental activity takes place below the level of our conscious awareness. More than 99 percent of what goes on in a calculator—hundreds, perhaps thousands, of operations—takes place offscreen. In both cases, only the end result is visible.

Thousands of "mental modules" in the unconscious carry on most of our lives for us, somewhere outside our consciousness. "The mind consists of a number of innate, domain-specific cognitive modules controlling such activities as language and visual perception, hardwired in the nervous system," writes clinical psychologist John F. Kihlstrom. These specialized subsystems of our brain regulate eating, breathing, memory, movement, and all the myriad other processes of our minds and bodies.

When someone tells us the sky is blue, we know instantly what it means, and never give the "why" a second thought. But during the space of half a second, specific mental modules apply our knowledge of language to the sounds, while simultaneously scanning our memory for each word's main meaning. Then, in less than the blink of an eye, the sense of what is being said pops into our minds almost before the speaker has finished talking.

Hard as we try, we cannot perceive or control our unconscious's activities. For, as Kihlstrom says, "they operate outside of conscious awareness and voluntary control," where "we have no conscious access to their operations." That's why scientists call it the unconscious.

Our unconscious performs many vital roles. It is the repository of our memory, experience, decisions, and everything that makes us *us*. The unconscious also monitors our body for signs of illness and disease; scans our minds for conflict and distress; assesses our environment for danger and threats; and relays and interprets perceptions, sensations, and feelings.

For our conscious mind to handle all that, as well as its own tasks of awareness, thought, and response, our brains would have to be more than 100 times larger. And so would we—to carry our boulder-sized heads around. Like the dinosaurs, our nerve impulses would take so long to travel from our heads to our limbs that we'd have become extinct millennia ago.

SOURCE: John F. Kihlstrom, "Cognitive Unconscious," *Science*, September, 18, 1987; Betsy Carpenter, "Stalking the Unconscious," *U.S. News & World Report*, October 22, 1990.

It's Smarter Than You Think

Feel dumb? Wish you had more brain power to bring to bear on your problems? Don't worry, you've got a secret genius on your side—your unconscious. It's a lot smarter than your conscious, according to research by psychologist Pawel Lewicki.

Lewicki proved not only the existence and power of the unconscious, but also how astonishingly "smart" it is. Volunteers pushed buttons corresponding to the apparently random appearance of an *X* on a computer screen. Although the volunteers were not informed of it, the X was actually following a very complex pattern determined by 10 interacting rules.

To see if participants could consciously figure out this pattern on their own, the researchers offered a $100 reward to anyone who did so. But no student collected, although several tried. Yet as they continued to play the game, each student's response time quickened, and they began to "instinctively" choose the spot where the X appeared. These students' unconsciouses, Lewicki concluded, had succeeded where their conscious minds had failed.

It may sound unbelievable—but it's true. Your unconscious is not only smarter than you think. It's smarter than you can (consciously) think.

SOURCE: Daniel Goleman, "Your Unconscious Mind May Be Smarter Than You," *New York Times*, June 23, 1992.

They Remember It Well

Can we remember our own births? Once scientists judged it impossible. Now there is increasing evidence it's true. Babies are fully conscious and aware at birth, according to pre- and perinatal psychologist David Chamberlain, Ph.D. And under the right conditions women and men can recall their entry into the world as vividly as they do last night's dinner.

Under clinical hypnosis in offices and laboratories, people have described in detail everything they saw, heard, and experienced during and immediately after their own births. At first, many scientists felt infant brain structure wasn't developed enough to retain birth memories. But Chamberlain and his associates won converts when they provided independent accounts from parents, relatives, and medical personnel that confirmed birth memories in almost every detail.

In the future, pleasant music and soft voices may be mandated in delivery rooms, Chamberlain suggests. Doctors, nurses, and parents will make an effort to maintain a positive, harmonious atmosphere throughout the birth process. As long as newborns are going to be fully aware of their entry into the world,

Chamberlain says, we might as well make their arrival as pleasant as possible.

SOURCE: Chamberlain, *Babies Remember Birth*.

It's Not the Devil's Fault

We don't make most of our own decisions or choose most of our own responses. We don't even determine most of what we think, feel, or want. Our unconscious does it for us.

Studies of brain cancer patients at the Dartmouth Medical School produced startling evidence that we can remain completely unaware of our actual motivation for an action, even while we're in the midst of carrying it out. In one study, researchers showed the word *walk* to the right eye of a patient whose left and right brain lobes were separated. The man promptly stood and left the testing area. When asked why, he told researchers he was "thirsty and going to get a Coke." The man had no conscious knowledge of the unconscious impulse that had actually motivated his behavior.

The many "conscious" processes research shows are controlled by the unconscious include:

· What we feel.
· What we think.
· How we act and react.
· The decisions we make.
· What we pay attention to.
· Who we love and who we hate.
· How we interpret the world and events around us.

If you have difficulty believing your unconscious determines much of what you think are your conscious thoughts and actions, you're not alone. Psychiatry professor Joseph Weiss, Ph.D., says, "It is generally assumed that human beings cannot carry out unconsciously the same kinds of intellectual activities they perform consciously, such as making plans and assessing risks. Yet," he continues, "studies indicate that, in fact, people can unconsciously think, anticipate consequences, and make and carry out decisions and plans."

The good news is, you can relax. What ever goes wrong is your unconscious's fault. The unconscious made me do it! may replace the old catch phrase, The devil made me do it!

SOURCE: Betsy Carpenter, "Stalking the Unconscious," *U.S. News & World Report*, October 22, 1990.

The Kid at the Switches

On what does our unconscious base its decisions? Mostly on what we believed as children about the way the world works and what is and is not possible in reality. Psychologist Robert G. Crowder of Yale University says 150 years of research have confirmed this view.

"Conscious perception is the product of unconscious inferences based on the individual's knowledge of the world and memory of past experiences," Crowder believes. No matter what we learn consciously later in life, the beliefs we form in childhood are more powerful. They form the basic operating system (the DOS if you will) of the biocomputer we call our minds, and all subsequent programs run within their parameters.

Studies have proven that childhood beliefs operating in our unconscious determine our stance toward life; what we think is possible and what we think is real; what we think we can and cannot do; what we think we should and shouldn't do; what we perceive and how we perceive it; our attitude toward politics and religion; and much of our interaction with other people. This discovery, that so many of what we had assumed were our adult decisions are really based on our juvenile perceptions and understandings of the world, lends new meaning to the biblical statement that "a child shall lead them"; and may explain the sorry state of so many "adult" institutions.

SOURCE: John F. Kihlstrom, "Cognitive Unconscious," *Science*, September 18, 1987; Bruce Bower, "Gone But Not Forgotten," *Science News*, November 17, 1990.

Our unconscious belief systems even prevent us from noticing facts that contradict them. One University of Arizona experiment demonstrated that when someone expresses ideas we disagree with, what they are saying triggers "negative memory modes" that cause our perceptions to focus in on the speaker's undesirable attributes. We do notice the positive elements about them and what they are saying, according to psychologists W. R. Kunst-Wilson and R. B. Zajonc, who conducted the study. But our unconscious places more emphasis on their negative aspects and the negative aspects of what they have to say. A similar process was found to minimize negative aspects of ideas and people we like.

It's no wonder we think we are right so often.

SOURCE: Kilstrom, "Cognitive Unconscious."

Unable to Face the Truth

"Control freaks" scoff at the existence of the unconscious. They claim they are fully in charge of all their own thoughts and actions. According to a study by Oxford psychologist Anthony Marcel, many people reject the suggestion that their unconscious exerts a greater influence over their lives than their conscious mind.

In the study, Marcel flashed a word on a screen so fast participants were unaware they had seen it. They then were given a list of words and asked to check the one most closely associated with the word they had just been "thinking" about. Although most of the women and men involved picked a word associated with the word on the screen, they were certain the screen had been blank. When Marcel questioned participants carefully, to make sure they hadn't seen the word, many walked out in a huff, angry because he kept pestering them about a word that hadn't been there.

SOURCE: Anthony Marcel, "Conscious and Unconscious Perception," *Cognitive Psychology*, Vol. 15, 1983.

OUR CREATIVE UNCONSCIOUS

Where Do They Come From?

Novelists are always asked where they get their ideas. Psychologist Ernest Rossi, Ph.D., says they come from the same place everyone else gets them: the unconscious mind, which he believes is the wellspring of all human creativity.

Rossi says we all have moments when creative ideas or insights bubble up into consciousness from their source in the unconscious. "These are the happy moments when we grasp the solution to a vexing problem, suddenly have a new perspective, or are hit with a flash of inspiration," he says.

People have bestowed many names on the wellspring of our creativity: the muse, a totem, the inner voice, the soul, the observing mind, God, the creative unconscious, the higher self, spiritual guide, the anima, and countless others. Whatever we call the experience, Rossi claims, its causes are always the same: "Your normal waking consciousness—what psychologists term the executive ego—relinquishes control, allowing the inner, creative parts of your mind-brain to come forward with new patterns of understanding and meaning."

Yet in the course of our rushed daily life, this creativity breaks through to our waking consciousness only occasionally. Often the signals our inner muse sends us are so subtle that, between the clamoring demands of work, personal commitments, family life, chores, and other concerns, we fail to recognize them. These creative inspirations can take myriad forms: thoughts, feelings, visual images, sounds, voices, even physical and visceral sensations.

The muse, as many poets have attested, apparently speaks in different ways to different kinds of people. "The important thing is to discover your own natural style of inner accessing," Rossi says. His prescription for discovering the way your creative unconscious signals you is simple. Just stop, relax, and take half an hour off. At the end of that time, you'll find you've experienced an abundance of creative inspirations.

SOURCE: Rossi, *20-Minute Break.*

You're One Too

Most of us don't think of ourselves as creative. We assume creative people must have enormous IQs. But highly successful authors, painters, musicians, scientists, and other creative types are no smarter than anyone else, according to psychology professor David Simonton, Ph.D. After numerous studies, Simonton was unable to discover any relationship between intelligence and creativity. On the other hand—considering the current state of popular writing and the arts—perhaps Simonton's results aren't all that surprising.

SOURCE: Simonton, *Genius, Creativity, and Leadership*.

Gift of the Gods

Creativity has long been regarded as a gift of the gods. But cheer up—creativity isn't limited to a favored few. Research shows you're as creative as any genius, says psychiatrist Ruth Richards, M.D. It's part of your birthright as a human being and hardwired into all our brains.

Richards sees creativity as a necessity we evolved to enhance human survival. Creativity, Richards claims, lies at the heart of our ability to adapt and to change. We're being creative when we learn how to perform a new job, for example, or change our plans at the last minute.

David Henry Feldman, a developmental psychologist who conducts creativity studies at Tufts University, concurs. Not everybody can be Beethoven, Feldman says. But all humans, by virtue of being dreamers and fantasizers, are creative. "They are always transforming their inner and outer worlds," he says.

If creativity is a gift of the gods, it's one they seem to have bestowed on all of us.

SOURCE: Leslie Dormen and Peter Edidin, "Original Spin," *Psychology Today*, July/August 1989.

Not Very Surprising

Most of us lose our creativity when we're young. Children's drawings, stories, and play show creativity develops quickly in early childhood, claims Harvard creativity researcher Howard E. Gardner, Ph.D. But tests show that by age seven, most of us loose the creative urge.

It generally takes only a year in the educational system to discourage grade-schoolers (and the adults they later become) from relating to their creativity. This loss of creativity is not very surprising, says professor Mark Runco, founder of the *Creativity Research Journal*, considering what happens to children in the school system. "We put children in groups and make them sit in a desk and raise their hands before they talk," says Runco. "We put all the emphasis on conformity and order, then we wonder why they aren't being spontaneous and creative."

SOURCE: Paul Chance and Joshua Fischman, "The Magic of Childhood," *Psychology Today*, May 1987; Leslie Dormen and Peter Edidin, "Original Spin," *Psychology Today*, July/August 1989.

Four Steps to Creativity

We have all felt the surprise and excitement that come when the solution to a difficult problem suddenly "pops" into our minds. But for most women and men such moments are maddeningly rare. Instead, we find ourselves wishing creative insight happened more often and that we could call on it whenever we needed it.

Now you can! Creativity researchers have discovered four steps common to all recorded experiences of creative insight:

1. Preparation, intently thinking your way through every aspect of the problem.
2. Incubation, letting go of the problem with your conscious mind, and turning it over to your unconscious.

3. Illumination, suddenly when you least expect it, your creative unconscious will supply the answer.
4. Verification, seeing if the idea works.

Millions of ordinary women and men, not to mention artists, scientists, inventors, and business leaders, have used these four steps to incubate the ideas that transformed their lives, and their pocketbooks.

SOURCE: Harman and Rheingold, *Higher Creativity*.

The Age of Genius

We tend to picture geniuses as youthful prodigies. Better add some lines of experience to that picture, and a touch of gray at the temples. Surveys show most of the world's celebrated geniuses spent at least 10 years mastering their chosen field before producing their fabled masterpieces, reports psychologist Howard Gruber.

Einstein is considered to have been a young genius because he formulated the theory of relativity when he was 26; but he had actually begun working on the problem at age 16. Mozart had been writing music for more than a decade, when at the ripe old age of 22 he penned what critics consider his first mature works. Gruber's research suggests a caution for self-styled young geniuses: Don't expect fame overnight—it's a 10-year wait.

SOURCE: Lesley Dormen and Peter Edidin, "Original Spin," *Psychology Today*, July/August 1989.

Mistakes: The Key to Genius

The secret of most geniuses' success lies in their failures. Geniuses aren't successful because they succeed so often, but because they fail so often. "Great geniuses make tons of mistakes," according to studies cited by Dean Simonton, Ph.D.

If these conclusions are right, the main difference between successful geniuses and the rest of us is that geniuses act on their ideas and inspirations more often. They know every idea they have can't be a winner and every project they attempt won't succeed. But they also know that if they keep generating ideas long enough, every so often one's bound to be a winner. Edison held over 1,000 patents, the book says, and most of them were not only forgotten, they weren't worth much to begin with.

SOURCE: Simonton, *Genius, Creativity, and Leadership.*

No Ivory Tower

Real estate agents hoping to sell ivory towers to geniuses are in for a disappointment. Despite what we've been taught, most geniuses don't need undisturbed peace and quiet to generate their creative output. The image of the hypersensitive artist who can only work in the isolation of an ivory tower is a myth.

Many creative types had their best inspirations in noisy, crowded environments. Dickens got the idea for *A Tale of Two Cities* while acting in a play. Noel Coward composed "I'll See You in My Dreams" in the midst of a traffic jam. Horror writer S. P. Somtow pens his epics while seated at the local mall.

Savvy real estate agents wishing to court the genius market are advised to skip the ivory towers. Instead, they should run ads for "A nice, noisy house under a freeway—ideal for creativity."

SOURCE: "That's Life," *Woman's Day*, May 12, 1992.

It's Never Too Late

Many of us feel strong creative urges in childhood, but put them off in favor of job and family. We don't realize how important they really are to us until suddenly in our late thirties or forties they return in full force, leaving us with a suffocating sense that we should have followed our hearts at the beginning. Usually we think it's too late, that creativity is a young person's game.

Research does show there are some areas of creative endeavor where age is a handicap. The best work in lyric poetry, mathematics, and theoretical physics usually comes from women and men in their mid-twenties and early thirties. All three fields are characterized by relatively early peaks, according to studies reported in *Handbook of the Psychology of Aging*, with somewhat steep descents thereafter.

But the same research reveals there are also creative fields that are "age-friendly," where maturity is a plus. Those stricken with the urge to create in their forties and fifties might be well advised to look toward writing, history, and general scholarship. The most acclaimed figures in these fields seem to reach their height at "a comparatively late peak . . . with a minimal, if not largely absent, drop-off afterwards," researchers say.

SOURCE: Birren and Schaie, *Psychology of Aging*.

It's True What They Say About Artists

People have always believed there is a strong relationship between genius and insanity. Psychiatrist Nancy C. Andreasen studied participants at a series of University of Iowa Writers' Workshops. She found creative artists are 400 percent more likely to have a mental illness than men and women in other professions. More than 40 percent suffered from manic-depression, 30 percent battled alcoholism, and in one study, 7 percent committed suicide before the year was out.

Andreasen's findings fit with research showing intense creative states are virtually indistinguishable from the manic state. An uncommon richness and intensity of emotional experience is triggered in both, along with a freeing of the unconscious processes and intense absorption in one's thoughts. Depression and mood swings may simply be the price some of us pay for our bursts of creativity.

SOURCE: Constance Holden, "Creativity and the Troubled Mind," *Psychology Today*, April 1987; Maisel, *Staying Sane*.

Our Daydreams and Night Dreams

THE FACTS ABOUT FANTASY

Dreaming Our Lives Away

If daydreaming your life away is a sin, it's one we're all guilty of. Up to half of the time, our minds are somewhere else. Daydreams occupy us 5 to 8 hours a day, 7 days a week. Over a year we'll spend 2,300 hours or more fantasizing; over a lifetime, at least 200,000 hours. That's more time than we'll devote to any other activity.

SOURCE: Klinger, *Daydreaming*.

And on Today's Program

Most of our daydreams are depressingly mundane, more concerned with what groceries we need to pick up for dinner than exotic, opulent flights of fancy. On those rare occasions when our fantasies do match the popular conception of daydreaming, they generally center around:

Money. Wealth and luxury are common daydream subjects among both men and women.

Power. Not only over others, but over our own destiny, for the freedom, respect, and ease it brings.

Sex. Biology ensures that suddenly, several times a day, uninvited sexual thoughts pop into our minds.

Reliving the past. Often we return momentarily to emotionally significant events in our lives, reexperiencing them with nearly their original intensity.

Rehearsing the future. Often we project ahead, planning how we will approach a difficult problem or fantasizing events we know will never take place.

These daydreams can be entertaining. At least half of them include color, movement, sounds, and a picturelike quality, according to dream researcher Eric Klinger. Draw the blinds and pass the popcorn, please!

SOURCE: Kottler, *Private Moments.*

Daydreams of the Rich and Famous

F. Scott Fitzgerald was right, the rich are different from you and me. At least their daydreams are, according to surveys by psychologist Leonard Giambra. Not only are the lives of the privileged more satisfying, so are their fantasies. The wealthy daydream about continuing success and future pleasures, and their fantasies contain less self-doubt, self-criticism, and guilt than those of other people.

SOURCE: Leonard Giambra, "Daydreaming: Religious, Economic, and Residency Influences," *Journal of Clinical Psychology,* Vol. 37, 1981.

Daydreams of the Poor and Obscure

The rich get richer and the poor get poorer. It's true not only with money, but with daydreams too. The disadvantaged have poorer daydreams than the wealthy. Vivid, frightening, hostile, and guilt-ridden daydreams were more common among disadvantaged

African-Americans than they were among middle-class white Americans, according to one Baltimore study.

SOURCE: Leonard Giambra, "A Black-White Comparison," *Journal of Personality and Social Psychology,* Vol. 42, 1982.

Efficient and Elegantly Ecological

Many of us consider daydreaming a waste of time. But daydreaming may actually prevent us from wasting our mental resources. We fantasize most when we have the most brain power to spare, according to studies by researcher Jerome Singer, Ph.D. Our brains are wired to keep ticking along, sorting information and generating possibilities, practical and impractical, through our every waking moment. When we have nothing else on our minds, daydreaming helps maximize the use of brain power that would otherwise be wasted. Rather than being a time waster, daydreaming appears to be an efficient, almost elegantly ecological, use of our mental resources.

SOURCE: Singer, *Inner World of Daydreaming.*

Why You Never Hear People Discuss Their Daydreams

People rarely share their daydreams. While friends think nothing of casually describing the most intimate details of their night dreams, chances are you can't remember a friend ever telling you about a daydream. Experiments conducted by Eric Klinger, Ph.D., revealed that, given the choice of describing a daydream or a real experience about the same subject, four out of five of us opt not to describe our daydreams. Participants were asked to share a real or fantasized achievement, something that happened with a friend, or a situation that aroused anger. An overwhelming 80 percent felt more comfortable describing an actual experience.

Why are we so willing to talk about our night dreams, and so reluctant to discuss our daydreams? Most people don't feel responsible for their nocturnal dreams, which occur when they are asleep. But they feel they must be responsible for daydreams, which occur while they are conscious. Since men and women are complex creatures with many conflicting needs and urges, some of their fantasies contrast with the image they wish to cultivate of themselves. When we find our self-image and our daydreams disagreeing, we believe there is something wrong with us, and hide our daydreams even from our closest friends.

SOURCE: Klinger, *Daydreaming.*

Rethinking Walter Mitty

Some women and men daydream a lot. Psychologists call them "fantasy-prone." Like James Thurber's character Walter Mitty, they experience great pleasure from daydreaming and they fantasize constantly, throughout almost everything they do and every encounter they have with others.

Heavy daydreaming was once considered a sign of immaturity and mental illness. However, when Ohio psychologists J.L. Lynn and Judith Rhue gave fantasy-prone participants a battery of psychological tests, they found the vast majority were normal, mentally healthy, well-adjusted individuals with successful careers and relationships. The Walter Mittys of the world, it turned out, fantasize so often because they have better quality daydreams. Perhaps because of a quirk in brain structure, what they imagine is far more vivid and intense for them than for most of us.

SOURCE: J.L. Lynn and Judith Rhue, "Fantasy-Proneness," *Journal of Personality and Social Psychology,* Vol. 53, 1987.

Daydreaming by the Clock

You can set your clock by your daydreams. That's the substance of research by psychiatrists Daniel Kripke and David Sonnenschein. Every 90 minutes we experience a biological urge to fantasize. Our biochemistry alters our mood and brain state so our thoughts become more vivid and fanciful. Ten to 12 times a day, whether we are talking to others, driving a vehicle, or facing a critical test of our abilities, the urge to daydream strikes. Which is why we so often find ourselves asking others to "Please repeat what you just said. I wasn't listening."

SOURCE: Antrobus, Singer, and Greenberg, "Stream of Consciousness," *Perceptual and Motor Skills,* Vol. 23, 1966.

What Kind of Daydreamer Are You?

We all have different daydream styles, writes Steven Starker, Ph.D., chief psychologist at the Veterans Administration Medical Center in Portland, Oregon. Researchers have discovered three main styles of daydreaming, and believe that each one reveals a great deal about the daydreamer.

Positive daydreamers. Have more vivid, upbeat, constructive, and enjoyable daydreams and night dreams, and a more positive attitude toward life; they rarely suffer from nightmares or insomnia, and their daydreams contain solutions to their problems more often than for other people.

Negative daydreamers. Have daydreams that are more laden with guilt, depression, anger, fear, anxiety, conflict, and failure; have a generally more negative attitude toward life; and are far more vulnerable to nightmares and insomnia.

Distracted daydreamers. Have daydreams that nervously jump around from one subject to another; they have the same trouble concentrating in their daily lives, perhaps because they become easily bored.

SOURCE: Starker, *F-States.*

The Power of Daydreams

Daydreams aren't just kid stuff anymore. Scientists have discovered that our fantasies have the power to literally transform our lives. The things we daydream about—walking, talking, making love—activate the actual brain cells involved in doing them.

Simply picturing ourselves feeling calmer or practicing a golf stroke can slow a racing heart or improve a score. Psychologists call this "guided imagery" or "mental rehearsal." Millions of people have used daydreaming to help them gain social skills, alter moods, sharpen athletic abilities, solve problems, prepare for difficult meetings, and improve their love lives. It's a form of self-improvement that doesn't cost a dime.

SOURCE: Klinger, *Daydreaming*.

It Doesn't Grow Hair on Your Palms, Either

Perhaps because daydreaming gives us secret pleasure, the puritanical among us have promulgated many myths about it. Scientific investigation has revealed these myths have no foundation. According to psychologist Steven Starker, research has overturned the following daydream myths:

Daydreaming can make you crazy. Repeated studies found psychiatric patients daydream no more than others; their daydreams reflect their mental illness, not the other way around.

Daydreaming can weaken your grip on reality. Experiments demonstrate that children who engage in games of "pretend" are better, not worse, than other children at distinguishing between fantasy and reality.

Daydreaming about things is so satisfying it weakens your motivation to work for them. In fact, the opposite is true. Psychologists have found that anticipation strengthens our motivation to have things.

SOURCE: Starker, *F-States*.

No Escape

The popular notion that daydreamers are trying to escape reality recently received a severe setback. A team of Louisiana communication researchers discovered that women and men with the greatest need to escape—the lonely, unhappy, and those in difficult circumstances—have the most unpleasant daydreams. Rather than escaping into fantasies of warm relationships and a better future or past, their imaginations were preoccupied with dismal projections of unsuccessful encounters and continuing failure.

SOURCE: Renee Edwards, J.M. Honeycutt, and K.S. Zagacki, "Imagined Interaction as an Element of Social Cognition," *Western Journal of Speech Communication*, Vol. 52, 1988.

Definitely Not Dreaming Their Lives Away

Many of us may think of senior citizens, especially the retired, as daydreaming their lives away. But fantasizing actually declines as we age, according to studies by Leonard Giambra. In one study, all participants who were forty-five still reported they engaged in significant daydreaming. Of participants who were sixty, only 75 percent still daydreamed. Only 27 percent of those who had passed seventy-five continued to fantasize on a daily basis; and 15 percent no longer daydreamed at all. Apparently it's the young, not the elderly, who daydream their lives away.

SOURCE: Leonard Giambra, Ph.D, "Daydreaming Across the Lifespan," *Journal of Aging and Human Development*, Vol. 5, 1974.

Not So Different After All

There is a point before sleep sets in when daydreams deepen, become more vivid, and for a period of time we pass into a unique realm of "hypnogogic" imagery, where we remain conscious while crossing the border between waking and sleep. Our daydreams and night dreams are more closely allied than we realize. There are "strong biological grounds" for supposing that the same brain mechanisms are involved in both waking and dreaming, says research psychiatrist Gordon Globus. Our night dreams, like our daydreams, are merely variations of the same state of conscious-ness. The only difference, Globus claims, is that our night dreams take place under the "special circumstances" of sleep.

SOURCE: Globus, "Causal Theory of Perception."

SEXUAL FANTASIES

Not Dirty Minded

We usually picture daydreams as lurid fantasies filled with erotic fulfillment and violent revenge. Most daydreams, however, are fairly humdrum. Sex occupies less than 1 percent of these fantasies; violence only a bit more. Why are we convinced our daydreams contain so much more eros and vengeance than is actually the case?

People remember things that arouse their emotions, explains daydream expert Eric Klinger, Ph.D. Our violent and sexual fanta-sies carry a higher emotional charge than those about the week-end's activities, and are more likely to come to mind when we think about daydreaming.

SOURCE: Klinger, *Daydreaming*.

Theirs Is Just Fine, Thank You!

Psychoanalysts once believed people who daydream a great deal about sex must be compensating for an unsatisfactory love life. But a survey of Missouri citizens suggests the opposite is true. Men and women with the most satisfying and active love lives had sex on the mind more of the time than those who rated their love lives less satisfying. These findings are supported by studies showing that when people commit to celibacy, the amount of daydreaming they do about sex begins to decline.

SOURCE: William Arndt, J.C. Foehl, and F.E. Good, "Specific Sexual Fantasy Themes," *Journal of Personality and Social Psychology*, Vol. 48, 1985.

Sexual Daydreams of Men and Women

From the enormous sales of romance novels to women and hard-core pornographic magazines to men, you might guess that their sexual fantasies would reflect similar themes. A survey by a team including psychologist William Arndt, Ph.D., found this to be the case. Romance and commitment are central elements in women's erotic daydreams, while explicit sexual activity and its variations play the dominant role in men's fantasies.

Arndt's study found that a woman's most frequent fantasies are:

- A man kissing her breasts.
- A man gently removing her clothes and making love.
- Being very glamorous and having sex with a very handsome man.
- Having sex where there is a risk of being caught.
- Attracting male attention at a party of the rich and famous.
- Wearing skin-tight clothes, with men staring at her.

A man most frequently daydreams about:

- Being excited by a woman's shapely legs.
- Kissing a woman's large breasts.
- Having a woman "forcing her intentions" on him.
- A woman telling him that she wants his body.
- Two women exciting him sexually.
- A party where everybody is having sex with everyone else.
- Watching a man and a woman having sex.

SOURCE: Ibid.

What Do the Kinky Daydream About?

Most people probably imagine the sexual daydreams of the kinky (those with unconventional tastes in sex) to contain an unending series of wild, perverse encounters and activities.

Psychologists Chris Gosselin and Glenn Wilson interviewed hundreds of men and women interested in unconventional sex. Those who enjoyed being spanked were preoccupied with scenarios of tanned cheeks and rosy bottoms; those who yearned for anal sex daydreamed of eager, cooperative partners; transvestites fantasized of dressing as, becoming, and being treated like women. But except for daydreaming more about their own particular fetish, their sex fantasies were monotonously unimaginative and average. The remainder of their sexual daydreams were no different than those of anyone else: intercourse with a partner they loved, intercourse with someone they knew but had not slept with, oral sex, watching others have sex, homosexual encounters, and other common fantasies.

SOURCE: Gosselin and Wilson, *Sexual Variations*.

That Helpless Feeling

For all our pretensions to sexual equality, few men or women fantasize about sexual situations where they and their partner make love as equals. Instead, more than 75 percent of us fantasize about forcing or being forced into sex. And the closer we get to orgasm, the more intensely unegalitarian our fantasies become.

It may disturb some to learn just how universal rape fantasies are among women. Almost 80 percent of those surveyed in a Masters and Johnson Institute study had such fantasies; and the figures were nearly the same for lesbians as for heterosexual women. What will surprise everyone is that far more men, 75 percent in fact, daydreamed about being forced into sex by women than about doing the forcing.

SOURCE: Klinger, *Daydreaming*.

The Grass Is Greener

Many heterosexual women and men daydream about engaging in gay sex. More than 25 percent of the men and 50 percent of the women in one Quebec study admitted fantasizing about an erotic encounter with a member of their own gender. Many heterosexuals even fantasized about gay sex during straight sex.

Turnabout seems to be fair play—at least in this particular case. Gay men and women also daydream about straight sex, according to the Quebec survey.

These fantasies do not necessarily represent a desire by gays to try heterosexuality or a desire by heterosexuals to try homosexuality, the authors of the Quebec study caution. The actual attraction may be the increased excitement and arousal we all experience when imagining novel and unusual sexual scenarios. Given the opportunity, both groups would probably prove very reluctant to practice in reality an activity that gives them so much pleasure in their fantasies.

Apparently, the grass is always greener on the other side of the sexual preference gap.

SOURCE: Claud Crepault, G. Abraham, and R. Porto, "The Erotic Imagination of Women and Men," *Archives of the Third International Congress of Sexologists,* Montreal: Quebec University Press, 1978.

Making Love in Stereo

It's something most partners do in bed during lovemaking. Some people think it's kinky, others are reluctant to admit to it. Most say it turns them on more than plain intercourse. Sexologists claim it's fast becoming the hottest new bedroom technique in our sexual repertoire.

We're having sex and thinking about sex, but the sex we are thinking about isn't the sex we are having. A study by psychologist Clark McCauley found that by the end of the first year of a relationship or marriage, three out of four men and two out of three women were daydreaming about sex unrelated to the sex they were having with their partner. These proportions continued to increase the longer the relationships continued.

Participants weren't fantasizing because of boredom with sex or because they no longer found their partner attractive. Having an exciting erotic daydream running through one channel of their brain, while the sensual input of making love ran through another, added an extra stimulus, a dash of spice. It was like making love in stereo.

Participants reported the most common fantasies they pictured during sex were:

· Making love to someone famous and glamorous.
· Oral-genital sex.
· A previous sexual experience or partner.
· Something wicked and forbidden.
· Activities partners refused to participate in.
· Being in different surroundings: a car, motel, drive-in, beach, woods, etc.

SOURCE: Eric Klinger, "What About Sexual Daydreams," *Psychology Today,* October 1987.

DREAM DATA

And It Doesn't Cost a Dime

Most of us experience the dream state six times a night. Over an average life span of 80 years, that works out to some 150,000 dreams or about 4 years of solid dreaming. If you paid to see that many motion pictures in a theater, it would cost you slightly over $1 million. Four years of cable television, on the other hand, would come to about $3,000. Either way, dreams are clearly your best entertainment value.

SOURCE: Siegel, *Dreams That Can Change Your Life.*

People Who Never Have Dreams

Although some people claim they never dream, they're wrong. They simply don't remember their dreams. EEG recordings reveal we all dream every 90 minutes throughout the night, every night of our lives. Those who believe they don't dream simply forget their dreams more easily than most.

SOURCE: Susan Chollar, "Dreamchasers," *Psychology Today,* April 1989.

How to Remember Your Dreams

If you have ever woken up with the vague impression of a wonderful dream you wished you could recall, or if you have trouble remembering your dreams, take heart. Psychologists have devised a simple four-step method that has helped millions remember their dreams.

1. Keep a pad and pen in a convenient location before going to bed.
2. When you wake up, without moving or opening your eyes, try to recall as much as you can of your most recent dreams.
3. Sit up slowly, allowing your body to remain in a relaxed, sleepy mode.
4. Open your eyes, reach for your pad and pen, and write down all that you can remember.

If you still have difficulty, give your dream recall muscles a boost by firmly telling yourself several times before falling asleep: When I wake up, I will remember my dreams. This suggestion acts directly on the subconscious, where dreams originate. Soon, you'll find yourself remembering your dreams far more often and in far greater detail.

SOURCE: Maybruck, *Pregnancy & Dreams.*

The Five Most Common Dreams

What do we dream about most? Are our dreams unique? Or are there common elements in all our dreams? According to dream researchers, five themes predominate in everyone's nightly excursions:

- Falling.
- Being pursued or attacked.
- Trying to perform an important task but failing repeatedly.
- Work and school activities.
- Sex.

It may be no coincidence that these themes appear so often in mass entertainment.

SOURCE: McCutcheon, *Compass in Your Nose.*

Blind Dreams

Many sighted people have dreamed about being blind. But what do the blind dream about?

Those born sighted dream with the senses that are most important to us: color, light, images, sound, and less frequently, touch or taste. Those born blind dream with the senses that are most important to them: touch and texture, hearing and sound, and flavor and scent.

Men and women who lose their sight during or after adolescence usually continue to dream visually as they always have. But those blinded as children generally lose the ability to "see" in their dreams as they mature.

SOURCE: "Blind Dreams," *Psychology Today,* January/February 1989.

Sleeping More and Enjoying It Less

The stereotype of the genius as a gaunt, pasty-faced individual with dark hollows under his or her eyes turns out to have a strong basis in fact. Geniuses look that way because their brains are busy working all night in their dreams. In fact, research shows that creative people and problem-solvers sleep longer. But they don't get more rest—instead, they dream more and wake up less refreshed. Albert Einstein, for instance, slept more than 10 hours a night.

SOURCE: McCutcheon, *Compass in Your Nose.*

Sleep on It

You *can* dream your problems away! Just tuck the subject that troubles you most under your mental pillow at night, and you may literally "dream" up the solution. That's the message of Willis Harman, Ph.D., who has spent years collecting thousands of accounts of great insights that came in dreams.

Robert Louis Stevenson dreamed the plot for *Dr. Jekyll and Mr. Hyde*. Mozart's masterpieces came to him during a dreamlike state of reverie in which he "heard" the music being played and merely scribbled it down as rapidly as he could write. Thomas Edison slept on the floor of his workshop and waited for inspiration.

University of Arizona researchers decided to put this anecdotal evidence to the test. They interviewed college students who were rated highly creative. An astounding 93 percent actually had been gifted with special insights during their dreams. Comfortingly, even 63 percent of students rated less creative received inspirations in their slumber.

SOURCE: Harman, and Rheingold, *Higher Creativity*.

Six Theories About Why We Dream

Why do we dream? And what, if anything, do our dreams mean? Dream researchers have been fighting tooth and nail over these questions for years. The following have emerged as the front-running theories in this hotly contested debate:

Coded messages from the subconscious. Views dreams as forbidden urges we can't bear to acknowledge consciously, so they slip forth in disguise during our sleep and must be decoded if we are to truly understand them.

Straightforward messages from the subconscious. Dreams are not in code and rarely about forbidden urges; they are straightforward messages about subjects we don't have time to think through completely during our waking hours.

A search for psychological equilibrium. Dreams are our mind's attempt to balance the inequities of our daily lives; if we have an encounter that makes us doubt our intelligence, we may have a series of dreams portraying us as alternately bright and stupid, until we reach emotional resolution.

Learning and memory storage. Dreams replay key experiences and information, reinforcing it in key sites where memories are stored in the brain; proponents point to thousands of studies showing dreaming plays a vital role in learning, especially when we acquire complex new skills.

A process of "unlearning." We dream in order to forget; the fragmentary images that give our nightly dreamscapes their shifting, surreal quality are stimulated as the brain erases unnecessary information from memory storage sites in the cerebral cortex.

Meaningless mental static. Dreams result when the random firing of brain cells while we sleep sets off a jumble of unrelated images and sensations; dreams have no underlying meaning and are not signals from the subconscious.

SOURCE: LaBerge, *Lucid Dreaming*; Edward Dolnick, "What Dreams Are (Really) Made Of," *Atlantic Monthly*, July 1990.

Will the Winning Dream Theory Please Stand Up?

The firing of a single nerve cell in a Rockefeller University laboratory may have spelled the end to decades of scientific quarreling over the nature and significance of dreams. Neuroscientist Jonathan Winson decided he might be able to resolve the controversy by establishing a definitive link between dreaming and memory. Aware that brain cells produce sharply increased theta waves during both learning and dreaming, Winson monitored several cells in the memory center of a rat's brain as it learned to run a new maze. One cell showed increased theta activity.

When the rat was taken out of the maze and returned to its cage, the brain cell that had produced increased theta waves returned to normal. Later that night, during dream sleep, the cell began to produce intense theta activity again. By tracking a specific brain cell involved in learning a task during the day to a dream later that night, Winson seemed to have answered one of the key questions of modern dream research: memory is indeed being stored during our dreams.

Since animals normally show increased theta rhythm when they are behaving in ways crucial to their survival, Winson believes dreams are a primitive brain mechanism for processing and storing information important to our personal well-being. Thus our dreams, though more a means of reinforcing memory than a vehicle for conveying messages from the unconscious, offer significant clues to our personal concerns and values, and through them to who and what we are.

SOURCE: Jonathan Winson, "The Meaning of Dreams," *Scientific American,* November 1990.

DREAM DILEMMAS

Dreams That Can Save Your Life

Dreams may be our early warning system for serious illness. A startling link between dream content and health emerged when psychologist Robert C. Smith of Michigan State University began studying the dreams of victims of heart attack, stroke, and other severe pulmonary illnesses. Long before the illness was apparent to patient or doctor, most victims had similar dreams involving common themes of death, disease, or disruption. The more frequent and frightening the dreams, Smith found, the weaker the pumping power of the patient's heart.

The dream symbols that warned women and men of approaching illness turned out to be stereotypically different. Men with failing hearts dreamed of death and destruction; women were haunted by nightmares of relationships doomed by forces beyond their control. As Smith was quick to point out, only about 5 percent of those who dream of death and separation are suffering from a serious illness.

SOURCE: Susan Chollar, "Dreamchasers," *Psychology Today,* April 1989.

Turning-Point Dreams

At moments of crisis or significant personal change, our dreams become more intense and vivid. These "turning-point dreams," as they are called, come most frequently at:

- The beginning of new relationships.
- The conception and birth of children.
- The ending of intimate relationships.
- During crisis and transition.
- Midlife transitions.
- Personal crisis: financial, natural disasters, crime victim, threat to a loved one.
- Injury and illness.
- Death of a loved one.

If we view the change as negative, or it causes us pain or fear, nightmares result. But turning-point dreams, claims Alan Siegel, Ph.D., who has spent decades studying them, can help ease our transition through crucial life passages by providing valuable clues to the successful resolution of their challenges.

SOURCE: Siegel, *Dreams That Can Change Your Life.*

How to Interpret Your Dreams

We all want to know what our dreams mean. Fortune-tellers and psychotherapists claim to be able to interpret them. Publishers have made fortunes issuing dictionaries of dream symbols.

"But the only person who can interpret your dreams is you. We dream in our own private code," says psychologist and dream researcher Gail Delaney. The most potent symbols in our psychological firmament have meaning only for us. "No one else can tell you what your dreams mean. Only you can know," she says.

To help decode the meanings in your dreams, Delaney offers a simple two-part process:

- Write a description of every image and event you remember from a dream.
- Ask yourself what real-life situation most resembles the one in your dream.

Delaney suggests using unlined paper and writing down ideas with lots of space in between. As one idea leads to another, draw a line between them. As connections develop, you should begin to see the patterns and meanings in your dream.

SOURCE: Kristin Von Kreisler, "The Dream that Haunts You," *Redbook,* April 1992.

Haunting Dreams

Have you ever been haunted by a dream? Have you dreamed the same sequence of events over and over, days, weeks, or even years apart? Dream researchers call these "recurring dreams," and most of us experience them at some time during our lives.

Recurring dreams can be uplifting and leave you exhilarated. Or they can take the form of nightmares that leave you drained and depressed. The bad news is that recurrent nightmares outnumber happy dreams by almost six to one. The good news is that recurrent nightmares are trying to tell you something.

Recurrent dreams are pointing to where it hurts, according to Dr. Edward N. Brennan, M.D., Assistant Professor of Clinical Psychiatry at Columbia University. And if we don't get the message the first time, "they will show you again and again and again," says Brennan.

SOURCE: Ibid.

Dreaming's Dark Side

Nightmares are the secret fear that haunts our dream life. They are dreaming's dark side. Nightmares don't just terrify us within the dream. We return to the waking world with heart hammering, chest tight, drenched in sweat, and flooded with fear.

We all have nightmares sometimes. A few of us visit night's dark realms frequently. "Sometimes we're more troubled than we realize," says dream researcher Milton Kramer, M.D. When "a problem seems insurmountable, the dream can turn into a nightmare." According to dream specialists, the most common nightmares and their meanings are:

Abandonment. Loss of a loved one.

Being chased. Feeling being stuck or threatened in your daily life.

Climbing. The desire to realize an ambition or anxiety about making a change.

Falling. Feelings of loss, insecurity, failure, or being out of control.

Killing an authority figure. The desire to break away from family, a job, a relationship, or a way of life.

Missing planes, trains, or buses. Fear of not progressing in life or of missing an opportunity.

Being nude. Fear of ridicule, exposure, and embarrassment.

Taking tests. Anxiety over a difficult challenge.

SOURCE: Rae Corelli, "An Awakening Debate" *Macleans*, April 23, 1990; Linda Leuzzi, "Nightmares Can Be Good for You," *Ladies Home Journal*, March 1990.

Nightmare-prone

Most of us have heard of people who are accident-prone. These are individuals, first identified by insurance companies, who seem to attract disaster. Now there's evidence that some people are "nightmare-prone." The dark terrors of the dream world come swarming in on these hapless men and women nightly.

Although nightmare-prone people are otherwise healthy physically and mentally, they have what psychiatrist Ernest Hartmann terms "thin emotional boundaries." This means they are more open and sensitive, and become more easily and deeply involved in relationships than most people. Their sensitivity may also make them more creative. Hundreds of studies have proven that artistic and creative people suffer from more than their fair share of nightmares.

SOURCE: "No More Nightmares," *Prevention*, November 1992; Linda Leuzzi, "Nightmares Can Be Good for You," *Ladies Home Journal*, March 1990.

Pregnancy and Dreams

Expectant mothers dream more. And their dreams are frequently unpleasant and disturbing. The physiological changes and the psychological stresses that accompany pregnancy provide fertile soil for nightmares and night terrors, according to dream researcher Patricia Maybruck, Ph.D. Six fears, each intimately connected with a woman's own pregnancy, shadow expectant women's dreams:

- The baby will be deformed or die.
- Being an inadequate parent.
- Losing her mate.
- A difficult delivery.
- Losing emotional control.
- Financial difficulty.

Pregnant women can take heart. Maybruck's research shows these dreams are produced by normal anxieties and are not prophetic.

SOURCE: Maybruck, *Pregnancy & Dreams*.

No More Nightmares

You can transform nightmares into sweet dreams. That's the message of Barry Krakow, M.D., a sleep researcher at the University of New Mexico. A simple new technique called "imagery rehearsal" has proved to be nearly 100 percent effective in banishing bad dreams. In one study, women and men who had been terrorized by nightmares for almost 25 years eliminated them completely in just a few weeks.

Krakow's imagery rehearsal involves learning to "incubate" positive dreams in which dreamers master frightening nightmares. Those suffering from disturbing dreams are asked to:

1. Write a summary of a nightmare you'd like to change.
2. Describe the way you would like to see the situation reversed.
3. Visualize this new dream for a few minutes each night before going to sleep.

"What's amazing about the rehearsal technique is that it didn't just make their bad dreams go way, it actually made the people feel better overall," says Krakow. Participants were no longer afraid to go to sleep at night, slept better, and felt more rested the next day. "It's such a simple technique but it works," Krakow says.

SOURCE: Krakow, *Conquering Bad Dreams.*

Lucid Dreaming

In the midst of a vivid experience, some element strikes us as incongruous, and we suddenly become aware we are dreaming. Stephen LaBerge, Ph.D., a leading authority on so-called "lucid dreaming," taught subjects, whom he called "oneironauts" (dream astronauts), to recognize when they were dreaming. Then in a feat that rivaled the first humans landing on the moon, LaBerge's subjects used a complex series of eye and body movements to send signals from within their dream worlds to observers in the waking world outside.

LaBerge believes we can reap a cornucopia of benefits from lucid dreaming: the elimination of nightmares, emotional and physical healing, anxiety reduction, decision making, and creative problem solving. Grandiose as these claims may seem, a University of Northern Iowa survey supports LaBerge's findings. Psychologist Jayne Gackenbach found lucid dreamers are less neurotic, less depressed, and have higher self-esteem and better emotional balance than other dreamers.

SOURCE: Jayne Gackenbach and Jane Bosveld, "Take Control of Your Dreams," *Psychology Today,* October 1989; LaBerge, *Lucid Dreaming.*

Learning Lucid Dreaming

Anyone can become a lucid dreamer, says Stephen LaBerge of the Stanford University Sleep Research Center. While only 1 person in 10 is a natural lucid dreamer, LaBerge has developed a simple process that has proved effective in helping tens of thousands learn lucid dreaming. LaBerge believes there are only two essential requirements for learning lucid dreaming: motivation and good dream recall.

LaBerge's four-step method for inducing lucid dreams includes:

1. When you wake spontaneously from a dream, go over all the details until you have them fully fixed in mind.
2. Before you go back to sleep, tell yourself firmly several times, Next time I'm dreaming I'll recognize I'm dreaming.
3. Visualize yourself inside the dream you just recalled, aware that you are dreaming.
4. Repeat steps two and three until the desire to remember your dream is firmly planted in your mind, or you fall asleep.

With a little practice, you should find yourself becoming lucid in your dreams.

Lucid dreaming may also be the ideal medium for overcoming nightmares. If you find yourself faced with a frightening situation in a lucid dream, simply face down the image that's threatening you. When that happens, LaBerge avers, frightening images vanish and rarely return.

SOURCE: LaBerge, *Lucid Dreaming.*

Our Gender and Sexuality

MEN AND WOMEN

What's the Difference?

Are women and men different? If so, how? And why? Cultural and scientific opinion has blown back and forth about the subject. For many years, apparent differences in the way the two genders thought, acted, and reacted were considered the innate result of their different biologies. More recently, culture was cited as the main cause of such differences.

But two decades of research into genetics, hormones, and brain structure have turned the tide. Scientists are almost unanimous: There *are* distinct differences between the genders, and nature, not nurture, is to blame. Jerre Levy, professor of psychology at the University of Chicago, spoke for the converted: "When I was younger, I believed that 100 percent of sex differences were due to the environment. Now, I am sure there are biologically based differences in our behavior."

On average, neuroanatomist Laura Allen says, men are more aggressive (and therefore more likely to be abusive) physically, emotionally, and sexually than women. On average, women are less aggressive (and therefore less likely to be abusive) physically, emotionally, and sexually than men. On average, men are more spatially and mathematically oriented than women; on average, women are more verbally and interpersonally oriented than men.

Though there is some evidence that the attitudes of parents and society play a role in influencing what makes men *men* and what makes women *women*, much more seems to be due to differences in:

Genetics. Genes determine whether fertilized eggs will develop as male or female; scientists believe as much as half of the differences between men and women may be genetically programmed.

Hormones. Sex hormones have an enormous influence over our behavior; when women are given male hormones, body hair increases, voices lower, aggression increases, and so does libido; and when men are given injections of female hormones, breasts and hips develop, while libido and aggressiveness decrease.

Neuroanatomy. Differences in the brain structures of women and men may explain the advantage of men in space perception, mathematical ability, and mechanical problems; and the advantage women have in verbal ability and memory tasks.

Researchers caution that these differences are purely statistical—that there is such a wide range of variation among individuals in both genders that some women have higher levels of aggression than most men, and some men have greater verbal and emotional skills than most women.

SOURCE: Christine Gorman, "Gender and the Brain," *Time*, January 20, 1992; Hooper and Teresi, *3-Pound Universe*.

Men: Traveling Light

Handbags—men would rather be caught dead than carry one. They even ridicule women who rummage for a moment in their bag to find the pen they asked for. So most men travel light, right? Wrong—their secret is out. Men might find they would look less ridiculous carrying purses than they do walking around with the bulging pockets they sport now.

A survey of men ages twenty-five to fifty-seven found males stuff so much into their pockets it's a miracle they can move. Most men had six or more items from the following list in their pockets: breath freshener, sports page, condoms, stamps, hair gel, keys, wallet, glasses and sunglasses, baseball cap, road map, gum, address book, mini flashlight, and a Swiss army knife.

Toting such a heavy load in your pockets is also dangerous to your health, says chiropractor Frank Castella. "When men sit, their billfold can cause the pelvis to tilt forward," he warns. "And adding weight to jacket pockets can throw your back out of alignment."

SOURCE: "First Impressions," *First*, February 10, 1992.

Hanging Out versus Hanging Together

Men and women—even the way they approach friendship is different.

Women "hang together." Their friendships are more intense, writes couples columnist Elizabeth Nelson. Relationships are important to women, who devote a lot of energy to cultivating them. Women like to spend as much time as possible with their friends, and can't imagine life without them. Women see friendships as a support network and as a way to keep a healthy perspective by bouncing ideas, joys, and disasters off someone who really knows you.

The male approach to friendships is much more casual. Men are content just to "hang out." Most men have friends they see from time to time, but it's rare for a man to be close to any of them. Even with close friends, says Nelson's husband and co-columnist Todd, men aren't as open about their emotions and worries as women are with other women.

Men actually value friendship as much as women do, Todd concludes. They just approach it differently. He points out that women's friendships have their drawbacks, too. "I've seen female 'best friends' start feuding, and suddenly the relationship's in the shredder." Men, he claims, are choosier and their friendships last for life.

SOURCE: Elizabeth Nelson and Todd Nelson, "Men and Friendship," *Glamour*, March 1990.

Why Men Don't (Usually) Have to Ask for Directions

Women have always wondered why men don't like to ask for directions. Now science may have the answer.

Men appear to excel at thinking in three dimensions. This may make them better at reading maps and certainly makes them better at visualizing their route, their location, and the way to their destination. Some sociobiologists believe this talent may be due to ancient evolutionary pressures related to hunting, which requires orienting oneself while pursuing prey.

As a result, scientists believe, some men need directions so rarely, that when they do need assistance, they become embarrassed because they are not used to asking for help.

SOURCE: Christine Gorman, "Gender and the Brain," *Time*, January 20, 1992.

The Mothering Instinct

Do women have a "mothering instinct"? Experiments at the University of Birmingham, England, appear to provide measurable physiological proof women have such an instinct—and men don't. Since the pupils of the eyes tend to dilate when we are interested in something and contract when we are bored, men and women were shown photographs of babies to gauge their interest. Whether the participants were single or married, childless or parents, the pupils of women participants dilated. But when the same photographs were shown to men, only married men with children displayed any interest. Apparently, men learn to be interested in children after having them. Women, however, seem to possess an innate "maternal" reaction.

SOURCE: Calder, *The Mind of Man.*

The Caretaker and the Lawgiver

Women and men don't just have physical and mental differences. They seem to have differences in values and perceptions as well. In a series of groundbreaking experiments, Harvard psychologist Carol Gilligan found that men and women have contrasting approaches to morality. The "caretaker perspective" was found predominantly in women and the "justice perspective" was found predominantly in men.

Asked to make difficult moral choices, women's concerns centered on helping others, providing care, preventing harm, and maintaining relationships. Men's concerns centered on abstract rules of fairness and justice, principles, and people standing on their own.

The justice perspective, Gilligan found, arises from a basic perception of the world as composed of separate individuals. Its focus is on protecting those individuals from unwanted interference in their rights through rules, rationality, and legal principles. Moral actions are based on fear of punishment or fear of authority, while moral decisions are based on following society's laws and the social order.

The caregiver perspective arises from a basic perception of the world as a network of interdependent people. Its focus is on reinforcing all the links in that network through human responsiveness. Moral actions are based on protection and compassion, while moral decisions are based on acting responsibly toward self and others.

Lawyers may be reacting to an intuitive sense of Gilligan's discoveries when they try to stock juries with women and exclude men in some criminal cases.

SOURCE: Gilligan, *In a Different Voice.*

Thirteen More Intriguing Differences Between the Sexes

There are hundreds of other differences between men and women, some subtle, some not so subtle. Here are a baker's dozen of the most intriguing:

- Women have a better sense of the future; they think more about it and plan ahead better.
- Men are harder to persuade than women.
- Women are more likely to express their emotions and to empathize with the emotions of others.
- Women are more likely to be anxious about failure and to blame themselves.
- Men are less likely to disclose personal information such as political and religious views, sexual activities, etc.
- Men are more prone to color blindness and left-handedness.
- Women are more sensitive to sounds and more agitated by loud noise.
- Men smile less often than women.
- Women have sharper senses: smell, taste, hearing, and touch.
- Men are superior at left-brain tasks (linear, logical); while women are superior at right-brain tasks (intuitive, creative).
- Women attempt suicide more often, but men succeed at it more often.
- Marriage increases the risk of depression for women but decreases it for men.
- Men commit 17 times more homicides than women.

SOURCE: Gerbrer, *Book of Sex Lists*; McCutcheon, *Compass in Your Nose.*

MORE GENDERS THAN TWO

How Many Genders?

Most of us think of ourselves as either female or male. Now biologists tell us we may be taking gender too much for granted.

The relationship between the sexes has always been so thorny that coping with just two genders has proved to be difficult enough for most people. But geneticists have discovered more than a dozen other "genders." According to psychobiologist Glenn Wilson, "there are not just two sexes, but a range of people who are male or female to a greater or lesser extent both anatomically and mentally."

Scientists have identified more than 12 different "intersex" states, in which male and female biological traits are mixed. Four out of every 100 people may be born "intersexuals" (there are an estimated 10 million intersexuals in the United States). In most cases, their chromosomes said they should develop as one sex, while their body developed as the other.

Normally men have XY chromosomes and women have two X chromosomes. But some women can have a Y chromosome and still be and appear overwhelmingly female, and some men can have two X chromosomes and still be and appear overwhelmingly male. Neither they, nor those who love them, have any doubt about their sexual identity or the slightest idea that their chromosomes and their bodies don't match.

It may be just as well that feminism has done away with gender-based social distinctions, like men opening the doors for women, or women walking on the inside of the sidewalk. With a dozen or more genders parading around, trying to keep special rules for each in mind would just be too much trouble.

SOURCE: Wilson, *Love and Instinct*.

The Other Kind of Transsexual

When most people think of transvestites and transsexuals, their minds naturally jump to images of men either dressed as women or surgically altered to become women. Often overlooked is a second kind of transvestite and transsexual: women who want to dress as men, live as men, pass as men, and sometimes even have their bodies surgically altered so they can perform sexually as men.

Probably the most famous case is that of Billy Tilden, the jazz musician who successfully passed as a male for more than 50 years, marrying and adopting children, until death and an autopsy uncovered the anatomical facts. Undoubtedly many "butch"-type lesbians, who act out an aggressively male role in dress and manner are driven, consciously or unconsciously, by the impulse to cross gender lines as well. Since sex change operations from female to male have only become possible relatively recently, and since women commonly wear male clothes in our society, no one knows precisely how many female-to-male transsexuals and transvestites there are.

Experts estimate that more than 25,000 males have undergone gender reassignment surgery to become female, and that about a quarter of that many women have had surgery to become males. But recently the number of women choosing gender reassignment has been increasing, according to Chris Moran, spokesperson for Professionals for Gender Awareness. Women are now seeking the operation at least half as often as men. Moran estimates that there are at least another 100,000 "pre-op" male-to-female transsexuals taking hormones and living part-time or full-time as women, and around 50,000 "pre-op" female-to-male transsexuals living as men.

SOURCE: Frank, "Women at Arms".

The Ideal Soldier

Men who object to women serving beside them in the military may have good reason. Women appear to make better soldiers.

Initially, male soldiers do start out with a somewhat greater advantage in upper-body strength, leg strength, power, body weight, and height. However, a West Point study reveals that women have a greater capacity for improving their physical condition than men. Women have also been found to endure starvation, exposure, shock, fatigue, and illness better. They have more acute hearing, and their sexual organs, being internal, are far better protected from injury. Women were even found to possess greater tolerance for heat because their sweat glands are spread over their body, rather than in a dense cluster like those of men, enabling them to sweat more efficiently.

Women may even be fiercer warriors than men. The late Dudley Sergeant, M.D., dean of the physical education department at Harvard, said his experiences convinced him that female combatants contradict the notion that women are inherently more pacifist than men. "The average, normal woman," he wrote, "is biologically more of a barbarian."

SOURCE: U.S. Military Academy at West Point, "Report on the Admission of Women".

Men—They're Always Going to Extremes

About male versus female genius—for males there's good news and bad news. First the good news: More men score in the genius class on IQ tests than women. Now for the bad news: More men also score in the mental retardation category than women.

This ties in with the general tendency of men to show more psychological extremes and abnormalities of every kind than women. The explanation, says sociobiologist Glenn Wilson, Ph.D., may lie in the fact that men lack a second X chromosome. Many geneticists believe the second X chromosome women possess duplicates all of the genetic information in the first and acts as a backup system, in case the first suffers damage or develops anomalies. Lacking this backup system, men are more vulnerable to the kind of genetic abnormalities that create genius, developmental disorders—and serial killers.

SOURCE: Wilson, *Love and Instinct*.

Who Did You Say Is Faking Orgasm?

Everyone knows women sometimes fake orgasm during sex; while some women fake it almost all the time. For many years, psychotherapists assumed women were simply trying to soothe fragile male egos. Now there is compelling evidence that the true explanation lies in the power of the myth that vaginal orgasm is a hallmark of female sexuality. The vaginal orgasm, according to feminist historian Sandra Stone, is the belief (promulgated heavily in romantic fiction) that most "real" women can experience pleasure and achieve a climax just from the friction and sensation of intercourse.

Recent surveys have confirmed that because they have bought into the myth of the vaginal orgasm, women often fake climaxes, even with men they know are secure in their sexuality. Studies at the Stanford University Gender Dysphoria Program suggest that the myth of the vaginal orgasm is so pervasive that even male-to-female transsexuals fake orgasms with their partners. Not one transsexual in a 20-year period would admit she had experienced sexual pleasure through any other means than intercourse. They also denied ever feeling sexual pleasure while living in "the wrong body," and would not even acknowledge that they had ever given themselves pleasure as "boys."

For everyone in the Stanford study concerned with femininity, Stone says, "Full membership in the assigned gender (female) was conferred by orgasm, real or faked, accomplished through heterosexual penetration."

SOURCE: Stone, "Empire Strikes Back." In *Bodyguards*, edited by Epstein and Straub.

THE BASICS

What's Love Got to Do with It?

A British government survey asked several thousand people to describe their most frequent motives for engaging in sexual activity. Their answers may not be surprising, but they are revealing.

Although society bestows its unreserved approval only on sex for love, love was only one among the many motives people gave for making love. Other reasons include:

- Feeling horny at the time.
- A strong physical attraction to their partner.
- Wanting to find out more about each other.
- Reassurance about their own attractiveness.
- Nothing more interesting to do.
- The desire to have children.
- The desire for closeness.

SOURCE: *Report of the Committee on the Operation of the British Sexual Containment Act*, 1978.

Good Long-Term Sex Is a Fantasy

Some couples seem to have the knack of keeping sex alive and vital throughout a marriage—others don't. The key, says Helen Kaplan, Ph.D., director of Cornell University's Human Sexuality Program, is to marry someone who looks and acts like your sex fantasy. Couples who managed this trick remained sexually entranced and excited with each other long after the passion had grown cold among others.

These couples said that when they met, they knew almost instantly that something special was going on between them, and that this feeling did not fade with either time or the physical changes that came with aging. Kaplan also discovered that even when one or both partners did not start out as the other's fantasy, but they were willing to fulfill it, the couple were able to capture and sustain the same kind of long-term sexual excitement in their relationship.

Perhaps Cinderella and Prince Charming did live "happily ever after."

SOURCE: Kaplan, speech, December 1990.

The Key to a Good Sex Life

Almost everyone wants a good sex life. Now a study by Captain David Hurlbert, clinical director of marriage and sex counseling at Dornall Army Community Hospital, may provide the key. Hurlbert found it wasn't the "how" of making love that determines the degree of an individual's sexual satisfaction, but his or her attitude toward sex. Couples with the healthiest attitude toward sex had the most fulfilling love lives. They also made love more often and experienced the highest frequency of orgasm. All rated themselves as looking forward to sex more than most people they knew, and reported greater satisfaction with their partners.

The Other Half of Sexual Expression

Our cultural stereotype, that men engage in sex for pleasure and women for love, turns out to be half right. These motives hold true when members of both genders are younger. But as they age, a curious phenomenon takes place: Men and women's reasons for having sex reverse. Women become increasingly motivated by the desire for physical pleasure, while men are motivated by thoughts of romance.

A combined Florida State University and University of Kansas study found that 61 percent of women in their twenties and early thirties gave love as their primary reason for engaging in sex, while only 22 percent would admit having sex for pleasure. However, pleasure became the main motivation for 43 percent of women over thirty-five, with only 38 percent claiming they had romance on their minds.

The survey also revealed a shift in the opposite direction among men. Almost 45 percent of men under thirty-five cited physical pleasure as their motive for having sex, with only 31 percent claiming love. But by the time they had passed thirty-six, the number of men who said romance was on their minds climbed to

50 percent, while the number who cited physical pleasure had fallen to 36 percent.

Psychologists say that physical pleasure and love are two halves of the same sexual coin. If that's true, then even though men and women both start out on one side of that coin, they each seem drawn to the other half of sexual expression.

SOURCE: Bruce Bower, "New Twist to Marriage and Mortality," *Science News*, October 27, 1990.

The Facts About the Facts of Life

Traditionally, parents are supposed to tell their children about the facts of life. However, American women and men of all educational levels, just don't know the facts about reproduction. One study found that today:

- Only 40 percent of women and 33 percent of men know that the most likely time for conception is about 2 weeks before the menstrual period.
- Only 39 percent of women and 28 percent of men know that the typical length of time during a month that woman can get pregnant is 2 days.
- More than 40 percent of women and nearly 50 percent of men don't know what ovulation is.

Considering this widespread ignorance, it may be time for parents to reinstitute the old-fashioned talk about the birds and the bees—or to vote for school sex education programs.

SOURCE: Dr. Joyce Brothers, "Column," *Los Angeles Times*, July 28, 1991.

What Will Drive You Crazy

If it really were true that self-gratification led to madness, 85 percent of the world's population would be stark raving bonkers by now. Surveys show that 94 percent of men and 80 percent of women masturbate, and that men do it about twice as often as women. Even infants do it, often several times a day. So do most animals; elephants, primates, canines, felines, even dolphins. Psychobiologists theorize that our urge for self-gratification, like so many near universal behaviors, may be hardwired into the brain. This would explain why animals prevented from masturbating become more moody and shows signs of stress. Apparently, parents should be admonishing their children to be careful, Not masturbating can drive you crazy.

SOURCE: Hooper and Teresi, *3-Pound Universe.*

BEYOND THE BIRDS AND THE BEES

Those Not So Sexy College Students

The old saw that college students think of nothing but sex is not true. In fact, a series of university studies revealed that only about 1 percent of the average college and university student's daily thoughts concern sex. Of course, that still means that the typical college student thinks of sex about 40 times a day.

SOURCE: Klinger, *Daydreaming.*

Anger or Ardor

Anger has long been thought to heighten desire. The image of two lovers quarreling violently, only to change moods in an instant and throw themselves passionately into each other's arms is familiar to everyone. But which is really stronger, anger or ardor?

A University of Houston study found anger reduced both arousal and sexual desire in male students. The angrier the males became, the less they responded sexually to the presence of provocative, attractive young women or to visual erotica. Rather than heightening their ardor for these young women, anger reduced it.

SOURCE: A. Bozman and J. Beck, "Effect of Anger on Arousal in Male College Students," *Archives of Sexual Behavior*, February 1991.

Cheaper Than Buying a Book

People often speak of being carried away by sex. Apparently they are right. One of the vital functions of sex is to carry us away from the here and now, according to psychologist Mara Adelman of Northwestern University.

We all inherited from our nomadic ancestors a strong need for excitement and diversity. Both are vital to our mental and physical health. Without this stimulation we become dull, sluggish, far from our best.

Like great music and a great story, passion and Eros help us transcend the mundane world around us and fulfill our need for excitement and novelty.

SOURCE: Mara Adelman, "Sustaining Passion," *Archives of Sexual Behavior*, October 1992.

Sizing Up Promiscuity

Are men and women natural cheats or do we really want true love? The answer, according to sexologist Jules Older, may lie in new understandings about how the difference in size between males and females of the same species (dimorphism) influences sexual behavior. When males and females are about the same size and shape, as with the gibbon, they tend to be strictly monogamous. But when there are significant differences in size, as with the elephant seals who keep harems with as many as 48 mates, species tend to be highly polygamous.

Men and women are moderately dimorphic (men are 8 percent taller and 20 percent heavier than women). Older calls this moderate dimorphism nature's joke on us. As a result, he believes, we are equally monogamous and equally polygamous, and we find ourselves torn by the conflict between the two opposing urges. So no matter how much we love our partner, we all have an occasional yen for others.

SOURCE: Jules Older, "Mother Nature's Dirty Tricks," *Los Angeles Times*, March 12, 1988.

Cold-Hearted Lovers

There may be some truth to those songs about cold-hearted lovers. Some people are physiologically unable to return romantic love. Only the problem isn't with their heart, it's with their pituitary gland. Our feeling of strong attachment toward another (scientists call it pair-bonding) is rooted in the pituitary. When it is damaged or alteration occurs, the hormones and nerve pathways controlling these feelings are disrupted. Those who have suffered malformation, disease, or injury to the pituitary are unable to feel the intense yearning to be with another that is the hallmark of love. "These people can show affection," notes Johns Hopkins University researcher John Money, Ph.D., "but most of them will never experience pair-bonding, the phenomenon most of us call falling in love."

SOURCE: McCutcheon, *Compass in Your Nose.*

What You Hate About 'Em Is What You Love About 'Em

Something about heterosexual men seems to leave their sex partners feeling ambivalent. Those who have relationships with straight men—straight women, bisexual women, and transsexuals—told interviewers that they found many traditionally masculine qualities such as aggressiveness and dominance both distasteful *and* arousing. They cited the ambivalence this created as an important factor in heightening the sexual excitement they experienced during encounters with traditional males.

SOURCE: Morin, "Four Corners of Eroticism."

The Sexual Peak

Many people talk about the "ultimate orgasm." Psychologist Jack Morin has spent years charting them. Suddenly, during sex, Morin writes, "all the crucial elements coalesce—the partner, the setting, an unexpected twist of luck or fate" come together. During these peak sexual experiences, love becomes so much deeper, more profound, and more physically and emotionally intense that something close to the core of our being has been touched.

The interviews Morin conducted convinced him that five elements interact, in combination or separately, to trigger a peak sexual experience:

- Intense attraction.
- Longing and anticipation.
- Violating prohibitions.
- Searching for power.
- Overcoming the fear of loving.

Sexual arousal, Morin says, whether love or lust, reaches its maximum intensity when there is enormous attraction pulling us toward our partner, and one or more obstacles standing in our way. Peak sexual experiences result when those obstacles, and our ambivalence, give way to passion.

SOURCE: Ibid.

Foot Fetish

Some of us find feet erotic. We like to touch and kiss our lover's feet and have our own touched and kissed in return. For years psychologists thought this was fetishistic, and attributed it to childhood imprinting. Neuroanatomists have a different view: They say that the desire to give and receive erotic pleasure through the feet results from brain structure and is a natural, normal impulse unless carried to extremes.

According to Dr. Vilaynur Ramachandran, neuropsychologist at the University of California at San Diego, the areas in the somatosensory cortex receiving and sending signals from our feet and our genitals are very close together. Sensations sent from the feet can easily be received by the brain cells designed to signal erotic pleasure from a somewhat higher locale. This would explain why some people become turned on when their feet are stroked, and others become ticklish if touched around the thighs.

SOURCE: Sandra Blakeslee, "Missing Limbs, Still Atingle, Are Clues to Changes in the Brain," *New York Times*, November 10, 1992.

And It's Legal, Too

Lots of us go on eating binges after an unhappy love affair. Chocolate is usually the poison of choice. Men typically gobble store-bought chocolate bars, while women seem to prefer theirs imported and exotically wrapped.

Although they probably don't know it, rejected lovers with a penchant for chocolate are taking the right drug for what ails them. Chocolate is loaded with phenylethylamine, a chemical that creates a happy, slightly dreamy feeling by stepping up our body's heart rate and energy levels, writes science journalist Marc McCutcheon. Ironically, phenylethylamine is the same chemical our brains secrete to create the dreamy sensation these brokenhearted lovers experienced when they first fell in love.

SOURCE: McCutcheon, *Compass in Your Nose*.

Mating and Marriage

ATTRACTION

Who Attracts Us?

Long before we meet our mates, we have an exact idea in mind of the person we want to share our lives with, according to psychologists R. H. Stretch and C. R. Figley. So what do we look for in potential partners? Intelligence, shared values, mutual interests, character, personality?

In one experiment, Stretch and Figley gave male and female college students detailed descriptions of the personalities and intelligence of a number of potential dating partners. The students were asked to select the candidates they most wanted to date. These candidates had been carefully screened beforehand so that their intelligence, values, and interests would match those of many of the students. The students were also supplied with photographs of their potential dates.

When the results had been tabulated, the candidates the students were most eager to date weren't chosen for intelligence, common values, or personality. It was how "good-looking," "beautiful," or "handsome" they were that counted. The more highly students rated the attractiveness of a potential date, the more they wanted to go out with that person.

SOURCE: R. H. Stretch and C. R. Figley, "Predictors of Interpersonal Attraction in a Dating Experiment," *Psychology*, Vol. 17, 1980.

You're Too Good (-Looking) for Me, Dear

We may all want to date the most attractive partner we can find, but given the choice, research shows, we often lack the courage to approach those we consider exceptionally good-looking. Experiments conducted in four singles bars found that men actually made fewer passes at women they considered beautiful than they did at women they rated of average attractiveness. Apparently, the more attractive we perceive someone to be, especially in comparison to ourselves, the more likely we are to feel they will perceive us as unattractive. This fits in with a number of complaints therapists have recorded from extremely attractive people, that they are rarely asked out on dates.

SOURCE: D. S. Glenwick, L. A. Jason, and D. Elman, "Physical Attractiveness and Social Contact in the Singles Bar," *Journal of Social Psychology*, Vol. 105, 1978.

What They See in Each Other

What turns on men and women? Surveys conducted by psychologist H. S. Budge, Ph.D., yielded two surprising results: First, that men and women judge the physical appearance of members of the opposite sex on the basis of a very small number of features; and second, their findings overturned a number of long-standing cultural myths about what men and women find attractive in each other.

The surveys listed a tempting menu of 44 physical attributes, from toes to eyelashes. But only a few turned out to be important. For men the most important things about a woman's appearance were: (1) weight, (2) face/features, (3) height, (4) hands, (5) figure, and (6) teeth. What women found most attractive in men was: (1) face, (2) hair, (3) silhouette, (4) shoulders/arms, and (5) height/voice.

Women are said to be less concerned with a potential partner's looks and more concerned with his character and values. But women chose face and biceps as what turned them on most about men. Men are reputed to be inordinately influenced by a woman's beauty. Yet, the men only rated a woman's face second and her breasts and figure fifth. Weight came first by a significant margin. Both men and women reported that a potential partner's face was extremely important to them, with more than 50 percent of both groups voting it the most important.

SOURCE: Budge, *Dimensions of Physical Attractiveness*.

The "Perfect" Face

Just what comprises the "perfect" face? In the West, at least, scientists think they have the answer.

In a number of tests involving European-Americans, men and women were asked what they thought were the ideal features in a member of the opposite sex, including: hair color and texture, face shape, nose profile and width, mouth and lips, and skin tone. For most white women the ideal male face turned out to be square and have a Roman nose, brown hair, and tan skin. For most white men, the ideal female face was heart- or pear-shaped, with a narrow or pug nose, full lips, and fair skin. Tests of other ethnic groups in the U.S. and Europe have produced similar results.

SOURCE: E. Wagatsuma and C. L. Klienke, "Ratings of Facial Beauty by Asian-American & Caucasian Females," *Journal of Social Psychology*, Vol. 29, 1979.

Boob Theory Goes Bust

Men are supposed to be crazy about women with big breasts, an impression reinforced in part by their group behavior around well-endowed females. But when it comes to actually choosing partners, most men prefer a moderate bustline. In dozens of tests conducted with a wide variety of men, breasts that were unusually small or large were perceived as a turnoff.

SOURCE: T. Horvath, "Physical Attractiveness: The Influence of Selected Torso Perimeters," *Archives of Sexual Behavior*, Vol. 10, 1981.

It's True What They Say About Girls (and Boys) Who Wear Glasses

Dorothy Parker may have said "Men seldom make passes at girls who wear glasses," but there's no sexism involved. The feeling is mutual: Women also seldom make passes at boys who wear glasses. Studies conducted by psychologist Robert Terry have proven that glasses do have a detrimental effect on others' perceptions, and ratings, of the wearer's physical attractiveness.

People who wear glasses are perceived as having less interesting personalities, although paradoxically they are perceived as being more intelligent. Ironically, the same people were described as sexy and fascinating when photographs of them without glasses were shown to a different group of test subjects. Apparently, men do make passes at girls who wear contacts (and vice versa).

SOURCE: R. L. Terry and D. L. Kroger, "Effects of Eye Correctives on Ratings of Attractiveness," *Perceptual and Motor Skills*, Vol. 42, 1976.

I Just Love Your Sense of Humor (or Lack Thereof)

We all know a sense of humor is vital to attracting a mate. Now science has proved we're right, but not in the way we think. It's not whether someone has a sense of humor that draws us to them—it's whether they share the same sense of humor we do.

Psychologists Bernard Murstein and Robert Burst surveyed 30 college-age couples to determine the relationship between sense of humor and what attracted them to each other. All the participants were asked to rate the humor of 25 cartoons, comic strips, and jokes. Then they were given a related questionnaire focusing on why they had selected their partner.

With these couples, it wasn't the presence or absence of a sense of humor that worked the magic. It was having similar senses of humor—or lack of same—that brought and helped keep them together. Murstein and Burst believe our sense of humor plays a more critical role in our lives than we generally realize. Our sense of humor (or even its absence), they claim, "is indicative of many things: values, interests, preoccupations, intelligence, imagination, and needs."

SOURCE: Bernard Murstein and Robert Burst, *Journal of Personality Assessment*, Vol. 49, No. 6.

COURTSHIP
The Facts About Flirtation

Flirting is good for you, and it's making a comeback. Relationship therapist Sonya Rhodes claims it's healthy for a woman and man to assess their desirability by flirting. Sometimes flirtation is serious and meant to lead to sex. But most often flirting is nothing more than a game, Rhodes writes, a pleasant time-passer that leaves participants feeling stimulated, alive, and desirable. The bantering humor of flirtation also helps lighten the sexual tension that arises when a man and woman find each other sexy.

The best flirts, according to magazine editor Louise Lague, are personal without being anatomical. Acknowledging that you have seen and appreciated the other person's secret self can be an enormous turn-on for them. People who are shy and quiet worry they're perceived as dull; they respond strongly when someone they find attractive notices their wit. Individuals who are a barrel of laughs worry that others think they are airheads; they light up immediately when a member of the opposite sex notices their serious side.

But flirtation doesn't necessarily require words. People flirt through smiles, direct eye contact, listening intently, or a touch while talking.

Handled correctly, Rhodes writes, there is an unspoken understanding, acknowledged through eye contact, that the flirtation is sexual without being seductive. Flirting merely says, I've noticed you, you're a sexy person, and under different circumstances I'd swoop you right off to bed.

SOURCE: Sonya Rhodes, "Go Ahead—Flirt a Little!" *McCall's*, January 1992; Louise Lague, "Flirting," *Glamour*, March 1990.

The Dark Side of Flirting

Flirtation is harmless when you stay within bounds. But because sexual attraction underlies flirtation, men and women frequently find themselves in a misunderstanding. Relationship counselor Sonya Rhodes has discovered seven warning signs that flirtations are taking you into dangerous territory:

- Do you keep thinking about someone you've flirted with?
- Do you play out affairs with someone you are flirting with in your head?
- Do you flirt on a regular basis to feed your self-esteem or only with special people?
- Do you ever have an embarrassed "morning after" feeling after a flirtation?
- Do you realize the effect flirtation has on someone who is sexually attracted to you?
- Do you send signals that could be presenting yourself as a potential accomplice in an affair?
- Do your flirtations prompt a sexual response?

Flirting can be fun, for those who follow the rules. But for those who carry it too far, or fail to heed the signals, what is intended as a light flirtation can lead to deeper involvement on the part of one or both parties, resulting in trouble and heartache for everyone involved.

SOURCE: Sonya Rhodes, "Go Ahead—Flirt a Little!" *McCall's*, January 1992.

You Believe in a Long *What*?

Long courtships went out with grandmother's high-button shoes. But new research suggests the old gal may have known her stuff, after all. In one Kansas State University study, a long premarital acquaintance was found to be a common factor in relationships that were still working after a quarter of a century.

The optimum length of these courtships seemed to be two years or longer. The Kansas researchers surveyed four groups of women: those who before marriage had dated or lived with their husbands (1) less than 5 months, (2) 6 months to 1 year, (3) 1 to 2 years, and (4) more than 2 years. Women in the last group reported the most satisfactory married lives.

The study concluded that the longer couples knew each other before marriage, the more time they had to determine whether they were truly compatible. Longer courtships also allowed pairings that were destined to peak early and then fade, time to burn themselves out, sparing both members the emotional turmoil of an unhappy marriage.

Evidently there is more to the old saying, "Marry in haste and repent at leisure," than most people realize.

SOURCE: Vincent Bozzi, "Courtship Counts in Marital Bliss." *Psychology Today*, April 1986.

The High Cost of Dating

Knights once paid a high price in blood and danger to win a fair damsel. Modern knights just pay a high price.

Even for adolescents, love doesn't come cheap anymore. In New York, a typical high school date costs about $60. Even a modest date for adults in Los Angeles can run to $175 or more, if you include dinner, concert tickets, parking, nightcap, and tips (and that's not including child care costs).

Why are we willing to spend such an extraordinary proportion of our income on dating? Couples counselor Tina Tessina, Ph.D., believes dating is so important to us because the outcome involves so many vital intrapersonal issues such as sex, acceptance, rejection, and marriage. Dating's importance, she says, is proved by the anxiety it arouses, the money both women and men spend on it, and the many subinstitutions it helps support:

movies, concerts, restaurants, valentines, and the cosmetic industry.

SOURCE: "Dating Dilemmas," *Teen*, October 1990.

Bye-Bye Courtship

Dating and courtship may be on the way out. Today's teens don't carry books for their sweethearts or share milkshakes at the soda fountain. The old girlfriend-boyfriend relationship is breaking down, writes Martha Toche, national editor of *American Demographics*.

Teens no longer ask for a date to a movie or a concert. Instead they just show up, usually in a group. The new courtship ritual for teens is traveling in packs anywhere they can hang out and buy soda, blurring the line between dating and friendly activities. At school, girls and boys are simply together a lot: studying, working, and playing. Expect this new style to transform adult dating habits too, Toche warns, as today's teens mature and carry the "new dating" through college and then to life as adults. "It's going to take time," she claims, but watch for "these trends to percolate through society."

SOURCE: Ned Zeman, "The New Rules of Courtship," *Newsweek Special Issue*, Summer/Fall 1990.

Who's Chasing Whom?

Evolutionarily speaking, the old folk saying "A man chases a woman until she catches him" turns out to be true. It's women who do the choosing when it comes to mating and marriage. According to sociobiologist Robert Trivers, Ph.D., women, not men, play the central role in natural selection and determining the future of the human species.

When the burdens of reproduction fall unequally on males and females, Trivers says, whomever bears the greatest burden, usually the female, ends up deciding the sexual success of the other. When a female carries the overwhelming reproductive burden (as they do among humans, with prolonged pregnancy and childhoods), she screens males carefully, often selecting those her genes tell her will make the best mate. As a result, much male behavior (more than men might willingly admit) is the result of males trying to appear to be what females want them to be.

What qualities do women look for in potential husbands? Trivers writes that the evolutionary evidence suggests they are guided by four criteria:

- The ability to provide significant resources or services, such as food or protection.
- Genetic superiority—healthier, smarter, more talented, stronger, more successful.
- Aesthetic traits—looks, physique, artistic ability.
- Their ability to reject other undesirable males.

Trivers's conclusions have been backed up by the largest cross-cultural study of human mate preference ever conducted. More than 10,000 women from 33 countries were surveyed, representing a wide variety of cultures and social situations. More than 97 percent of the time, women had chosen men for characteristics such as increased earning capacity, ambition, and industriousness.

SOURCE: Trivers, *Social Evolution*.

Marriage Fever

People in an unseemly hurry to wed may have contracted what psychologists call "marriage fever." Most of us fall in love and want to get married at some time in our lives. But marriage fever is the result of an all-consuming obsession with getting married for marriage's sake.

Any number of factors can trigger marriage fever: a biological clock that is about to run out, loneliness, a long series of temporary relationships, even a sudden nostalgia for the family scenes and feelings of childhood. But, according to magazine editor Jennifer Farbar, when a woman begins clipping pictures of wedding gowns and a man begins planning clever ways to propose—and neither is seeing anyone special at the time—then marriage fever has probably struck, and it afflicts men and women alike.

Human nature being what it is, as soon as one party starts wanting marriage, the other often becomes ambivalent. When the siren call of love is only heard by one, feelings are bound to be hurt. Men usually react with anger, Farbar writes, while women tend to feel rejected. In the grip of a serious case of marriage fever, rather than accept a turn-down as final, both men and women are likely to redouble their efforts to convince a reluctant person to say, "I do."

SOURCE: Jennifer Farbar, "Marriage Lust: When Only One of You Has It," *Mademoiselle*, March 1992.

The Look of Love

How can you tell if what you feel is really love and not just a case of marriage fever? Look in the mirror. That's the essence of advice given by David Baron, deputy clinical director of the National Institute of Mental Health. When romance strikes, a host of chemicals and hormones are released that enhance our physical condition and make us more attractive. "When people are in love," says Baron, "they blush, their voice cracks, and their pulse races."

Another reason for this miraculous physical transformation is that when people feel better about themselves, they look better. "When we fall head over heels, we become cheerful, optimistic confident, and energetic," says psychologist Dorothy Tennov.

Our blood pounds, our eyes sparkle, our skin glows—no wonder they call it the look of love.

SOURCE: "Love Makes You Beautiful," *First*, February 10, 1992.

No More Heartaches

Love won't be as painful in the future, claims Arthur B. Shostak, professor of sociology at Drexel University. As the median age of the population increases, Shostak expects to see more mature courtship behavior. People will take their time finding mates and getting married. They'll also be less likely to feel it's the end of the world when a relationship ends.

SOURCE: "The Great American Date," *Glamour*, February 1990.

MARRIAGE: THE BASICS

The First Year Is the Hardest

It's true, the first year of marriage is the hardest. The initial period of adjustment to each other's differences often wrecks new marriages, according to psychologist Samuel L. Pauker. But only for those who enter it with an unrealistic view of what marital life will be like.

Pauker surveyed husbands and wives who had been married at least 10 years. Almost half reported serious difficulty during the first year of their life together. Significantly, the same group also said they found marriage to be harder than they had anticipated. Couples with the most unrealistic expectations of married life, Pauker concluded, were least successful in coping with its initial challenges.

Most women and men contemplating marriage fail to realize that relationships don't happen overnight but take time, agrees Howard Markman, head of the Center of Marital and Family Studies at the University of Denver. It helps if they are able to abandon the idea of instant compatibility. Couples need to understand that they will have to go through life making changes if they want a successful marriage.

SOURCE: Samuel L. Pauker and Miriam Arond, *The First Year of Marriage: What to Expect, What to Accept, and What You Can Change.*

You Seem So Distant, Dear

Wives often complain that their husbands seem "distant." These women are describing emotional distance—but it turns out that men also put physical distance between themselves and spouses when they are dissatisfied with the way a relationship is going.

Marital partners were asked to walk toward one another and stop when they reached what they felt was a comfortable distance for conversation in an experiment by psychologist D. Russell Crane of Brigham Young University. The greater the husbands' dissatisfaction with their marriage, Crane found, the farther they stood from their wives. Men whose marriages Crane rated "distressed" maintained a 25 percent greater distance between themselves and their wives than husbands in successful relationships.

SOURCE: "Gender and the Brain," *Time*, January 20, 1992.

Too Sensitive to Fight

Everyone knows that marital conflicts send many men fleeing. With the first sign that an argument is brewing, husbands beat a hasty psychological retreat, followed by a strategic physical withdrawal. Now researchers believe they have discovered why: Males are more sensitive than their wives and just can't handle the intense emotions fighting with a spouse stirs up.

Psychologist John Gottman, Ph.D., took husbands and wives undergoing marital counseling and attached them to equipment that recorded a wide range of physiological responses including skin conductivity, brain waves, and heartbeat. The recordings Gottman made clearly show that the men became more physiologically aroused during arguments than women.

The husbands' hearts beat faster, their brain waves became disturbed, they perspired more, and they became more anxious. These sensations are so unpleasant, Gottman concluded, that many men who become emotionally upset simply panic, becoming desperate to avoid an argument or potential argument. If these husbands are unable to escape physically, Gottman says, they stonewall with faces frozen and heads rigid, displaying no reaction to anything their wives say.

SOURCE: Hara Estroff Marano, "The Reinvention of Marriage," *Psychology Today*, January/February 1992.

When Women *Don't* Talk

What wives *don't* complain about is often a clearer indication of trouble spots in their marriage than what they do complain about. If a woman never mentions sex, finances, intimacy, or children, even when other wives are discussing them, you can be sure these are sources of intense marital anguish, according to couples counselor Sonya Rhodes.

Some wives conceal serious problems, even from close friends, because they are afraid of being disloyal, Rhodes says. Others want to present their marriage in the best possible light. But most frequently, women are reluctant to discuss real relationship hot spots because of the underlying fear that their marriage won't measure up to those of their friends.

Next time a husband's in the doghouse and doesn't know why, he might try asking his wife's friends what she *doesn't* complain about.

SOURCE: Sonya Rhodes, "The Hidden Dangers in Your Marriage," *McCall's*, September 1992.

The Secret of Marital Longevity—Part 1

What's the secret of marital longevity? What do wives and husbands who remain together for life do right that the rest of us do wrong? Psychologists Judy Todd and Ariella Friedman of the California State University, Dominguez Hills, Counseling Center decided to find out. They were certain men and women who had stayed wed over the long haul would have found solutions to many of the problems that cause other couples to divorce. But when Todd and Friedman surveyed those celebrating golden wedding anniversaries, the results were disheartening.

Most of the wives and husbands told the psychologist they were very unhappy and had been for years. All that held them together was the belief that divorce was wrong, no matter how bad a marriage might become. "We would get so sad at the end of the interview," Todd says, "that we wouldn't do another one for two days." Reluctantly Todd and Friedman concluded that many couples who remain with each other for life do so not because of any happiness or personal fulfillment they have within the marriage, but because they have rejected the idea of divorce.

SOURCE: Wilson, *Love and Instinct*.

The Secret of Marital Longevity—Part 2

Happily, Todd and Friedman's survey doesn't tell the whole story. A study of 351 couples who had been married for 15 years or longer painted a much brighter picture of togetherness. More than 90 percent of the wives and husbands interviewed by psychologists Jennets Laer and Robert Laer expressed satisfaction with their relationships. An astonishing 300 of 351 couples pronounced themselves happily married. Only 19 couples said they were unhappily married, while the remaining 32 were unable to agree on how happy they were.

When the Laers asked men and women with successful relationships why their marriages had worked out so well, the replies were illuminating. The seven most frequently cited factors were:

- My spouse is my best friend.
- I like my spouse as a person.
- We agree on aims and goals.
- My spouse has grown more interesting.
- We laugh together.

· We agree on a philosophy of life.

· We agree on how and how often to show affection.

Couples who share these qualities, the Laers feel, have a solid foundation on which they can build an enduring relationship.

SOURCE: Jennets Laer and Robert Laer, "Marriages Made to Last," *Psychology Today*, June 1985.

Blame It on the Man

How husbands handle conflict—especially whether they withdraw during arguments—determines the success or failure of most marriages. "Many people believe that the causes of marital problems are the differences between people, and problem areas such as money, sex, and children," says University of Seattle psychology professor Howard Markman. "However, our findings indicate it is not the differences that are important, but how these differences and problems are handled, particularly early in marriage."

By noting the way men handled disagreements in the initial stages of marriage, researchers at Seattle's University of Washington found they could accurately predict which couples would remain together and which would divorce. They called the degree to which the husbands withdrew during an argument the most important predictor of divorce. They believe the issue goes to the heart of contemporary marriages. Most women find it difficult to live with a man who walks out in the middle of a fight.

SOURCE: Hara Estroff Marano, "The Reinvention of Marriage," *Psychology Today*, January/February 1992.

Other Forms of Marriage

Marriage has always conveyed the image of a woman and a man living together in a monogamous relationship. But in the United States alone, the number of families headed by wedded heterosexual couples has fallen to 77 percent (50 million) and continues to decline. What about the remaining 23 percent (20 million families)?

Family Synergy of Los Angeles, which acts as an umbrella group for those living in alternative lifestyles, say they are in touch with people living in a variety of relationships, who define themselves as "married":

- Monogamous heterosexual relationships: premarital, postmarital, nonmarital, and celibate.
- Monogamous, committed gay and lesbian marriages.
- Open marriages.
- Bisexual marriages.
- Triadic marriages.
- Role reversal marriages.
- Dual-household marriages.
- Group marriages.
- Polygamous marriages.
- Polyandrous marriages.

In all these marriages, monogamy, or its pretense, appears to be the rule rather than the exception. But those unable or unwilling to practice it have a variety of alternative marital arrangements to choose from.

SOURCE: Tessina, *Lovestyles.*

IT HAPPENS TO EVERYONE

Intimacy Can Be Bad for Your Marriage

We all want intimacy. That's one reason we marry. Thousands of books, tens of thousands of articles, and countless television programs have promised to help us develop intimacy. Now there's evidence that full-time intimacy actually hurts relationships.

Emotional space and time alone are critical to a healthy self and a healthy relationship, says sex therapist Linda DeVillers, Ph.D. Intimacy is vital to self-growth and understanding, she says. But so is the freedom to develop unique aspects of ourselves and explore areas of the world outside that call to us personally. Lucky couples balance intimacy and freedom, granting each other the space and privacy that allow them to be close and merge.

SOURCE: DeVillers, letter.

The Seat of the Matter

Where wives and husbands sit when they go driving with other couples is a clear indicator of their economic status. Sociologists charted the seating habits of North American married couples and made some astonishing discoveries. Blue-collar couples prefer to keep their spouses by their sides. When white-collar couples go out, the husbands sit up front, with the wives in the back. Among the wealthy, the woman guest is likely to sit in the front seat with the host husband, and the male guest in back with the wife. But, when the wealthy head out in chauffeured limos, they reverse the working-class lineup completely: the wives sit up front while the husbands recline in back and talk business.

SOURCE: "Save a Seat for Me," *First,* February 10, 1992.

Marital Look-Alikes

People who choose their mates on the basis of physical appearance may be on the right track after all—one day you may look like the person you marry. According to psychologist Robert B. Zajonc, Ph.D., the old saw about marrieds growing to resemble one another is true. In a survey involving photographs of husbands and wives, those married 25 years or longer were perceived as more similar in appearance than younger couples.

Zajonc attributed this resemblance to evidence that when we are placed in proximity to others for long periods of time, we begin to unconsciously mimic their mannerisms. After years together, this can affect the way wives and husbands use facial muscles as well as their skin texture, the way they tilt their heads, and their expressions. Zajonc also found that the more marrieds resembled each other, the greater their happiness and satisfaction with the relationship. This could be perhaps because those who liked their mates tended to mimic them more, while spouses who were dissatisfied with their mates tended to avoid mimicking their behaviors.

SOURCE: Robert B. Zajonc, "Expectancy and Feedback as Independent Factors in Task Performance," *Motivation and Emotion*, Vol. 11, No. 4.

Marital Sex: It's No Big Deal

Sex may play a less important role in a satisfying marriage than many people think. A U.S. International University team asked husbands and wives to rank the factors they thought contributed most to wedded bliss. One of the phrases couples could have chosen was, A satisfactory sex life. Surpassingly, sex didn't even make most participants' top-10 list.

SOURCE: Jennets Laer and Robert Laer, "Marriages Made to Last," *Psychology Today*, June 1985.

A Unique Approach to Life Extension

Women who marry younger men live longer. A recent study reveals that women whose husbands are at least five years younger live significantly longer than average. Ironically, women whose husbands were at least five years older died significantly younger than average. If these figures are supported by subsequent research, insurance companies may soon be funding ad campaigns directed at selling women on the advantages of wedding younger men.

SOURCE: Bruce Bower, "New Twist to Marriage and Mortality," *Science News*, October 27, 1990.

Missing an Opportunity

More than 40 percent of all husbands and 20 percent of all wives expressed interest in mate swapping, according to a magazine survey of 4,000 couples. However, the institution of marriage is not the hotbed of immorality these figures make it seem. For all their brave talk, less than 4 percent had actually tried swapping mates, and only 1.5 percent traded mates with any frequency. Apparently switching partners with others is honored more in the breech than the observance.

SOURCE: Karlen, *Threesomes*.

What Parents Regret Most About Sex

Warning: Children have been proven to be hazardous to your sex life. Psychologists Carolyn Cowan and Phillip Cowan found that most childless couples still have as much fun in the bedroom as they did during the first years of marriage. But those who became parents reported a significant drop in sexual satisfaction.

The Cowans attribute the decrease in marital sex to the demands of parenting. Their findings may cast light on a recent "Dear Ann Landers" poll in which 70 percent of parents said that if they could live their lives over again, they would choose not to have children.

SOURCE: Grossvogel, *Dear Ann Landers*; Carolyn Cowan and Phillip Cowan, "Making the Most of Marriage," *Psychology Today*, December 1987.

Not Your Mother's House

Sex may suffer when children come into a marriage, but the house goes first. With so much of the day taken up by children and job, 42 percent of working mothers drop other activities to find time for their husbands, according to a magazine survey. More than 80 percent lower their standards of housekeeping, while friendships also go on the back burner for 51 percent. Despite all this corner-cutting, the demands of parenting were so time consuming that 75 percent of the women surveyed admitted they had to sacrifice much of the time they formerly spent with their husbands.

SOURCE: "Time-Poor Women: Housekeeping Goes First," *Psychology Today*, June 1989.

Signs of a Successful Marriage

With so few examples of successful marriages around, people have little to help them gauge how well their own is working. Are the problems they are having just the routine difficulties everyone encounters during married life? Is their relationship sound enough to last? Or, are there already indications that it cannot be, or is not worth being, salvaged?

Family therapist Tina Tessina, Ph.D., says that it is easy to tell if your relationship is working well or not. In a relationship with healthy dynamics, both partners can:

- Discuss problems and disagreements without fighting.
- Allow each other to have different opinions and styles.
- Recognize and acknowledge serious differences without laying blame or making accusations.
- Speak for themselves and make their wants known.
- Hear and understand each other, even during disagreements.
- Relax their normal roles when necessary.
- Find time to communicate on a regular basis.
- Work together as equals rather than engaging in power struggles.
- Embrace each other's change and growth.

Marriages without these qualities, Tessina says, may be facing troubled waters ahead.

SOURCE: Tessina, *Lovestyles*.

Therapies and Therapists

PSYCHOLOGY AT A GLANCE

Science or Silliness?

What's on your mind? The world's political situation? Urban crime? An insult you received in sixth grade? An unfulfilling relationship? Whatever you think and feel, and how and why you think or feel it, is the province of psychology.

Psychology is one of our newer sciences, little more than 100 years old. Some people even claim it isn't a science. Otherwise, they say, therapy's success rate wouldn't be so hit and miss. According to numerous surveys cited by Jerrold Maxmen, M.D., in *The New Psychiatry,* currently only one out of two clients shows improvement. Critics also point to the headline-generating crimes committed by those who have been under the care of therapists; the number of people who seem to stay stuck in therapy for years without improvement; and the ever-growing visibility of the mentally ill among the homeless on the streets.

What most people don't realize, says psychologist Tina Tessina, Ph.D., is that psychology is a very young science, barely out of its infancy. Medicine, biology, physics, astronomy, and most other sciences have roots reaching back thousands of years. By comparison, psychology is little more than 100 years old (professionals date psychology's origin to 1879 when the first psychological testing laboratory was founded at the University of Leipzig, Germany, by Wilhelm Wundt). Until then, religion held a jealously guarded monopoly (usually enforced with the rack and the pyre) on defining what went on in the human psyche, and why.

Psychology, or its popularizers, did overclaim its success rate at first, concedes psychiatrist Jerrold Maxmen, M.D. And they often leapt to incorrect conclusions in early attempts to unravel the way the mind works. But during the last two decades, this science of the mind has come a long way, uncovering many of the physiological and psychological processes that underlie our behavior, thought, and feelings. Best yet, Maxmen claims, psychology has begun to discover universal rules everyone can use for creating a more satisfying, fulfilling life.

SOURCE: Tessina, letter; Maxmen, *New Psychiatry.*

The Power Behind the Throne

Most of us think of psychology and therapy as synonymous. But therapists represent only the tip of the psychological and psychiatric iceberg. In order for therapists to treat us successfully, someone has to first research how and why the mind works. Behind each therapist, and each therapeutic success, stands an army of tireless researchers in numerous fields of psychology who helped develop the psychological insights which created that success. Among the most important fields of psychology and their areas of research are:

- **Abnormal psychology.** Mental illness, violence, war, sadism, criminal behavior, and all the other aberrant qualities of human behavior.
- **Biological psychology.** Building better balanced brains through chemistry (psychopharmacology).
- **Clinical psychology.** Applying theory to therapy in the therapist's search of a therapeutic result.

- **Cognitive psychology.** Thinking, concept formation, and problem solving.

- **Comparative psychology.** Psychologists compare the behavior, motivation, and reactions of animals with those of people.

- **Developmental psychology.** Childhood, adolescence, adulthood, old age; patterns, problems, turning points, and progress.

- **Educational psychology.** How we learn, how we can learn, better learning, and why we don't learn.

- **Experimental psychology.** Experiments, surveys, and studies to test theories about human behavior.

- **Physiological psychology.** Brain cell, brain structure, and brain chemistry; how they affect, create, and guide what we think, do, and are.

SOURCE: McWhirter and McWhirter, *Illustrated Encyclopedia; Compton's Encyclopedia.*

They're Easy on Your Pocketbook, Too

Talking it out for years with a therapist is passé. Psychotherapists have discovered a whole new set of roads to mental health. Today's innovative therapies are cheaper, often faster, and best of all, more fun. Even their names are fun:

- **Dream therapy.** Instead of waiting for the unconscious to send us signals in the form of dreams, uses dreams to send messages to the unconscious.

- **Imagery.** Harnesses the power of images to change body, attitudes, feelings.

- **Bibliotherapy.** The benefit derived from reading self-help books.

- **Occupational therapy**. Having something useful to do can make anyone feel better.

- **Recreational therapy**. Nothing's better for the ills of urban stress than a good, relaxing hobby.

- **Self-help and personal-empowerment groups**. By following a few simple steps, a group of average people can do themselves a great deal of good.

- **Hypnotherapy**. Using states of deep relaxation to create mild self-hypnotic states to overcome destructive habits and reinforce self-growth.

If you and your loved one aren't getting along—or if your life just seems a mess—you might want to head right down to a therapist's office and try out one of the new therapies. You can relax and enjoy yourself, knowing you're working hard to solve your personal problems.

SOURCE: Robson and Edwards, *Getting Help*; Heller and Henkin, *Bodywise*.

Putting Psychology to Work

Psychology isn't just good for helping women and men with low self-esteem or chronic depression. It's also good for what ails us in all the other important arenas of our lives: relationships, recreation, job, family, sex, and business. In fact, psychologists are hard at work in all of these areas, diligently unearthing the secrets of how each shapes our minds and is shaped by them:

Business psychology. How and why we do business; how to get others to do business with us; how we can best do business.

Family psychology. Moms, dads, kids, healthy and unhealthy interactions; generational patterns, grandparents, uncles, aunts, siblings.

Marriage. Why we love who we love; why we fall out of love; the various stages of love; how to make love work better and last; the physicality of love.

Industrial psychology. The colors, sounds, and environments that produce the most productive workplace; repetitive tasks; mental and physical limits; employee morale; work flow and efficiency; making life better for workers because it enhances the bottom line.

Social psychology. Making friends and enemies; forming groups; cultures, mobs, nations, and armies; teams; the way groups work, the way they affect us, the way we interact in them, and the way they conflict and cooperate with each other.

Sports psychology. Seeks to find the maximum mental leverage we can bring to physical competition and challenge.

Vocational psychology. The right person for the right job, and steering the wrong person away from the wrong job.

Though much progress remains to be made, psychology has helped improve and continues to improve our lives in all these arenas.

SOURCE: McWhirter and McWhirter, *Illustrated Encyclopedia; Compton's Encyclopedia.*

Express Yourself

Men and women have always found it easier to express themselves through dancing, singing, writing, painting, and all the other arts, than with words. In the hands of a skilled therapist, the arts can become a powerful therapeutic tool. These so-called "expressive therapies" include:

Music therapy. Playing and listening to music hath charms to soothe the savage client.

Art therapy. What we draw and paint reveals much of what we feel and are.

Dance therapy. When the body feels free in motion, our emotions feel free to express themselves.

Journaling. Get a whole new perspective on yourself and discover long-buried feelings as you commit your experiences to paper.

Crazy as it sounds, all these therapies have been shown to help make people saner. If psychologists are right, expressive therapies can be an express route to mental health for many people.

SOURCE: Robson and Edwards, *Getting Help*; Heller and Henkin, *Bodywise*.

THE TALKING CURE

Talking It Out

Talking it out—that's the age-old principle behind psychotherapy. You and your friends do it every time you settle down to gripe about your problems over tea, a beer, or during a phone-side chat. The only difference is that professionals are more objective and have (at least in theory) a superior knowledge of the secrets of successful living.

Like close friends, therapists have a knack for putting us at ease so that we let down our defenses and feel free to talk about personal problems. Their supportive, nonjudgmental manner makes it possible for us to discuss our most troubling emotions, upsetting events, embarrassing facts, and less than admirable behaviors. While we talk, our therapist is tuning in to our verbal and nonverbal communication: tone of voice, facial expression, and body posture. Many things we do offer telltale clues to the source and nature of our difficulties: issues and subjects we keep coming back to; what we don't talk about; the subjects that stir our feelings; and when what we are feeling doesn't match what we are saying.

Acting on these clues, the therapist draws conclusions about what's gone wrong in our lives and how things might go right. Then, when they sense we are ready for a fresh approach, therapists offer suggestions, hints, advice, and comments intended to help us find healing insights. "A valid insight is one that leads the clients to resolve personal problems and immediate life difficulties in a positive, healthy way," writes psychiatrist Jerrold Maxmen, M.D.

SOURCE: Robson and Edwards, *Getting Help*; Maxmen, *New Psychiatry*.

Group Grope

Group therapy, it turns out, can be easier on the pocketbook than therapy for one, typically costing each only a tenth to a third the price of individual therapy. A group of men and women gather once a week under the guidance of a therapist. During sessions they discuss their own difficulties and share their insights (often stingingly) on the problems of other members of the group. Members sometimes argue, react, and begin to discover their own relationship patterns. The group, in effect, becomes the therapist.

Some people believe this interaction between members makes group therapy superior to private therapy. They claim it provides the same insight into personal problems and a unique focus on our relationships with others, often the very source of the troubes that sent us into therapy. "The group is a laboratory for showing patients how they affect others, for offering advice on better ways of relating to people, and for experimenting with these behaviors," writes psychiatrist Jerrold Maxmen, M.D.

SOURCE: Maxmen, *New Psychiatry*.

Togetherness

Sometimes it isn't a person who's troubled. It's a relationship or a family. When that happens, therapists try to persuade all involved to enter therapy as a unit.

Couples therapy focuses on the difficulties women and men face in making intimate relationships work. "Most relationship skills are pretty hit-and-miss," says therapist Tina Tessina, Ph.D. "Also, people from different families have different expectations of what a relationship is and what actions show loving and caring. It's not surprising that so many couples have trouble making their relationship work." Couples therapy aids partners in acquiring expertise in problem solving, self-assertion, conflict resolution, negotiation, and clear communication.

Family therapy often begins with a troubled child. "Because many emotional problems in children are reflections of family problems, many therapists now 'see' the entire family," writes psychiatrist Jerrold Maxmen, M.D. The therapist attempts to help members identify and replace unhealthy patterns and ways of relating.

Apparently the family that visits shrinks together—stays together.

SOURCE: Maxmen, *New Psychiatry*; Tessina, *Lovestyles*.

The Software Is a Shrink

Computers have replaced people in many areas of life—now they're replacing shrinks as well. Dozens of computer programs offer to help solve your problems and provide healing insights.

Software can provide broad insights into our personality and character, according to a report in *Psychology Today*. Several programs incorporate the classic Minnesota Multiphasic Personality Inventory, which has been proven to produce accurate personality profiles of those who take it. But when it comes to healing and personal growth, software is not as accurate. Its effectiveness is hindered in large part by the inability of psychologists to develop standardized rules of therapy that produce consistent results.

Human therapists, on the other hand, are hindered by the inability of their patients to be completely honest about their thoughts and feelings. This is one area where computers have an edge, the report concludes. Studies show women and men consistently give more honest answers to a computer than to a real therapist.

SOURCE: "This Machine Wants to Help You," *Psychology Today*, February 1988.

Effective But Illegal

Research conducted at Vanderbilt University implies you may be able to analyze yourself just as effectively as any professional.

During the study, troubled individuals were counseled for six months by professionals with at least 20 years of experience. Counseling was also provided by nonprofessionals selected on the basis of warmth, trustworthiness, and interest in others. The report's conclusions, as reported by Bernie Zilbergeld, M.D., Ph.D., were eye opening: The nonprofessionals with no formal training proved as effective as professional healers. "Patients undergoing psychotherapy with college professors showed, on the average, quantitatively as much improvement as patients treated by experienced professional therapists," the researchers stated.

What many people overlook is that "all of us to some extent are experts on doing therapy on ourselves and others," writes Zilbergeld. Every day of our lives, he claims, we unknowingly give and receive what would be called therapy if it were performed by a professional. We are engaging in self-therapy whenever:

1. We tell ourselves to stop dwelling on the negative and accentuate the positive.
2. We reward ourselves on completion of a difficult or distasteful task.
3. We release explosive feelings through physical exercise or hard work.
4. We lie down, relax, and "space out" to good music, feeling calm and refreshed afterward.

(Professionals refer to these techniques as thought stopping, positive reinforcement, catharsis, and trance induction or deep relaxation.)

Our own efforts may not seem very impressive to us, but as the Vanderbilt study shows, they are remarkably successful much of the time. Some of us are better than others at administering self-therapy, but Zilbergeld notes that the same can be said of professionals.

There's only one drawback to self-therapy. It's illegal to practice therapy without a license in some states. But don't worry. If you don't turn yourself in, nobody else will.

SOURCE: Zilbergeld, *Shrinking of America.*

What Therapy Can and Can't Do

Many of us think of psychotherapy as a miraculous cure-all for emotional disturbance and personal problems. But talking therapy is effective for only some of the mental ills that plague us. Surveys show it works best for less serious, less persistent problems, such as reducing fear, raising self-esteem, resolving sex, marital, and family conflicts, and strengthening assertiveness. But many studies indicate there is also a host of psychological ailments for which seeing a therapist is not particularly effective, according to psychologist Bernie Zilbergeld, Ph.D. Among them are clinical depression, compulsive behaviors (with food, drugs, and sex, for example), schizophrenia, and hard-core criminal behavior. When it comes to some of the more serious illnesses, psychotherapy still has serious progress to make.

SOURCE: Ibid.

A Quick Fix

Often we fear to seek a therapist's help because we've heard psychotherapy is a process that takes years to complete. But studies at Palo Alto's Mental Research Institute prove short-term therapy produces the same results as treatment lasting 2, 3, 10, or even 20 times as long. Studies have shown that 10 to 25 sessions of intensely focused therapy generated the same improvement rate (75 percent) as long-term therapy. Many people around the world, Zilbergeld asserts, "are allowing themselves to be seduced until therapy becomes a way of life."

SOURCE: Ibid.

Dark Side of Therapy

Some people even believe therapy does more harm than good—at least in some cases. One out of every 10 men and women in therapy appears to get worse, according to surveys quoted by Bernie Zilbergeld, Ph.D. One reported that, "On the whole . . . it appears that 5 percent to 10 percent of patients or of marital or family relationships worsen as the result of treatment." Another study of group therapy participants found that 16 percent were worse off after the groups than before, and that their deterioration seemed a direct result of being in the groups.

But therapy has the power to harm only because it has the power to heal. Zilbergeld writes, "A moment's thought should be sufficient to indicate that a method powerful enough to produce positive change is also capable of producing negative change." Even Sigmund Freud, the founder of psychoanalysis, acknowledged the potential dangers of therapy when he asked one student: "If you can not do any harm, how can you do any good?"

SOURCE: Ibid.

A Pet Would Be Cheaper

When all is said and done, what benefits does psychotherapy actually produce? Summarizing the vast research into the effectiveness of therapy, psychotherapist Bernie Zilbergeld established that it had been proven to help ease fear and anxiety. The most important benefits of therapy, he says, however, are not behavior change but caring, comforting, and structuring. Of the other sources of these three forms of emotional support, marriage is most expensive, pets are extremely low maintenance, but dollar for dollar, a mother's love is unquestionably your best alternative.

SOURCE: Ibid.

Guess Who Needed a Shrink

In their writings, the great figures of psychotherapy seem models of rational, unruffled composure. But in their personal lives, they may have been as confused, self-destructive, and petty as the rest of us. Sigmund Freud, the father of psychiatry, was practically a textbook case, while his followers enacted out all the classic patterns of adolescent rebellion and sibling rivalry. It isn't possible to catalogue all the personal eccentricities and petty foibles of these pioneers of the mind—but even a brief summary of their careers reveals enough steamy neurosis and latent sexuality to supply the plots for half a dozen soap operas.

Freud—Sex Was at the Root of It

Sigmund Freud (1856–1939) was a physician who became interested in patients whose illnesses had no apparent physiological cause. His celebrated conclusion—that many of our physical and mental ills are caused by underlying psychological conflict between the conscious and unconscious—continues to shape psychotherapy 100 years later.

Therapist. Freud appeared to suffer from many of the aberrations he became famous for identifying in his writings. These included the rigid and uncompromising habit patterns of schedule, dress, meals, family, and work that characterize the neurotic.

Theory. Freud believed our minds are composed of three conflicting parts:

- **Id.** The primal, self-centered instincts (survival, sex, pleasure) that lie buried deep in the unconscious, beyond our control.
- **Superego.** Consciously learned parental and social

taboos (sexual restraint, moral codes, selflessness) against giving free rein to the self-centered urges of the Id.
· **Ego.** The self or personality, caught between the instinctive urges of the Id and the restraints of the Superego, attempting (with and without success) to channel the former (like sex) into socially acceptable forms (like courtship and dating).

When our Superego successfully balances the needs of Id and Ego, we are "healthy"; when it fails the result is psychological imbalance and mental illness.

Therapy. After noticing that people often reveal unconscious clues to their real concerns in dreams or as "slips of the tongue," Freud developed a technique called psychoanalysis. He used it to get clients to relax and "free associate," analyzing verbal clues for insight into the unconscious conflicts and unresolved instincts that he believed lay at the basis of their psychological problems.

Psychotherapy has come a long way since Freud first formulated his "psychoanalytic" theories, and the authenticity of his cures and research methods have been seriously called into question. But even his critics honor Sigmund Freud for his founding contributions to the "science of the mind."

SOURCE: Schultz, *Freud and Jung.*

Jung—Standing in the Shadows

Carl Jung (1875–1961), who was already interested in science and the mystic, turned to Freud's new psychoanalysis in his search for the secrets of the mind. He shared Freud's view that primal instincts strongly influence behavior but believed they were counterbalanced by a spiritual instinct that sought personal growth and a feeling of connection to something larger than the self. Jung believed mental illnesses began when men and women failed to fulfill all the aspects of their personalities.

Therapist. Jung was Freud's "favorite son," the designated heir who would become head of the psychoanalytic movement upon Freud's death. Ironically, their relationship played out one of Freud's most celebrated theories: the Oedipal conflict. This theory says that males have an inherited animalistic urge to slay and replace their fathers. Soon Jung was rejecting many of his father figure's doctrines and replacing them with his own. Twice during arguments between the two, Freud became so worked up that he fainted; he even accused Jung of harboring homicidal feelings toward him.

Theory. Jung's description of the unconscious was far more elaborate than Freud's and drew heavily from mystic traditions. In addition to a personal unconscious, there was a:

Collective unconscious. The few basic forms and feelings the brain perceives are reflected over and over again in our art, dreams, symbols, and myths (the mandala, the dream of flying, heroes and villains, mother love). Jung called these "archetypes" and felt they exerted a more direct and powerful influence on the unconscious (and hence conscious behavior) than sexual instincts.

Polarized unconscious. The conscious is outward and extroverted; the unconscious inward and introverted. When the first dominates, men and women have a tendency toward openness, sociability, and physical drive. When the second dominates, they have a tendency toward quietness, solitude, and thought.

Shadowed unconscious. We are so disturbed by the things we consider negative, bad, or even "evil" about ourselves that we force them out of our conscious minds into the unconscious. These repressed aspects of ourselves are called the "shadow."

Sexual unconscious. Most of us also repress the elements in our make-up associated with the opposite gender. Forced into the unconscious, these elements become the "contrasexual archetype of the ego" or "soul-image" (in men, the anima or female spirit; in women, the animus or male spirit). We fall in love when we find someone whose outward manner matches our soul-image, not realizing it is the need for union with our repressed male or female self we see in them, and not their real nature, that attracts us.

Therapy. Through exploration of the patient's dreams and fantasies, seeks to discover conflicting archetypes underlying the client's problems in order to trigger self-discovery and self-growth (and not just cure mental illness).

Jung traded Freud's mechanistic, deterministic model for a view of the mind as an organic, creative whole, unfolding to purposive ends.

SOURCE: Hampden-Turner, *Maps of the Mind.*

Freud's Followers

For more than half a century, Freud and his theories reigned supreme. Everyone who wanted to know anything about the mind made a pilgrimage to sit at the feet of the master. But like Jung, each turned rebelliously against Freud, replacing the theory of primal instincts as the wellsprings of human behavior with other theories which saw society, family, or culture as primary. Among Freud's most famous progeny, and the schools of psychology they founded, were:

Alfred Adler (1870–1937). The founder of individual psychology, Adler felt social experience was a stronger influence on behavior than the unconscious. He believed mental illness begins as an unsuccessful attempt to compensate for the feelings of inferiority a child experiences when it first compares itself to parents and other adults. Adler was the first to point out the role sibling order of birth plays in their personality development. Adler became the first male to suggest that what Freud identified as "penis envy" in females was probably envy of the power wielded by its possessor and not of the object itself.

Otto Rank (1884–1939). Stressed the importance of will. In Rank's eyes, the weak-willed, unable to assert themselves, became mentally ill. Rank believed anxiety-related illnesses began with traumas caused during birth by early twentieth-century obstetrical practices; his theories created a revolution in delivery room procedures.

Erich Fromm (1900–1980). Argued that freedom is frightening, and claimed that many people (and societies) followed dictators to escape the burden of making their own decisions. He drew a convincing catalogue of the various defenses and personalities women and men develop to cope with their fear of freedom. Fromm felt that in healthy families we evolve from dependence on maternal bonds as infants to increasing capacities for independence, while we grow from self-centeredness to increasing capacities for loving: first family, then neighbors, then humanity and nature itself. He believed psychology's highest purpose lay not in the treatment of mental illness, but in its potential for enhancing everyone's ability to live and love.

Karen Horney (1885–1952). Played out her own Oedipal role in the psychoanalytic movement. She claimed parents' attitudes and behaviors played a stronger role in forming personality than primal urges; believed mental illness was fostered by thoughtless, uncaring parents. Horney rejected many of Freud's theories regarding female sexuality and personality, particularly the concept of penis envy and the idea that women are inherently masochistic. Ironically her revisionism led colleagues to accuse Horney herself of suffering from penis envy.

Erik Erikson (1902–1979). An artist and teacher who became interested in the psychoanalysis of children. He believed that at each stage of development in life, we face a specific psychological challenge that we must resolve successfully for continued growth; failure to resolve the challenge results in mental illness. In infancy for example the challenge is choosing between developing a sense of trust (the world is a safe, warm place that is ready and willing to meet one's needs) and a sense of mistrust (the world is unsafe, cold, and withholding). Erikson believed healthy women and men have parents who helped them develop a strong sense of trust while retaining enough mistrust to keep them from being reckless.

SOURCE: McWhirter and McWhirter, *Illustrated Encyclopedia*; Robson and Edwards, *Getting Help*.

New Directions

As the new science of psychology developed, it began to reflect a pronounced American influence. The new psychologies were more pragmatic, aimed toward fitting emotionally disturbed men and women back into a productive society.

William James and functionalism. William James (1842–1910) developed the first distinctively American brand of psychology, which he called "functionalism." This method focused on studying the functions served by human thought and action. The mind was thought to adapt to disruptive events by seeking to return to its original equilibrium; failure to adapt led to mental illness. Functionalism's pragmatic bias won a wide following in the United States, where it led to an emphasis on testing abilities and aptitudes and the grading of individuals as "normal," "average," and "successful" or "unsuccessful."

Watson, Skinner, and behaviorism. Behaviorism was founded by John B. Watson (1878–1958) at the turn of the century, but brought to international celebrity in the 1960s through the writings and theories of B. F. Skinner (1904–1990). Behaviorists believed "mind" and "consciousness" were subjective states whose existence could not be scientifically proven. Psychology should concern itself with concrete, observable behaviors like speech, action, and reaction. Skinner believed that all behavior, including mental illness, was learned, and his therapies focused on changing the behaviors associated with mental illness, rather than the causes and cure of the illness. As with functionalism, behaviorism's pragmatism made it a major force in American psychology until the late 1960s, when researchers returned to the investigation of human thought as well as behavior.

Harry Stack Sullivan and interpersonal psychology. Harry Stack Sullivan (1892–1949) believed personality and mental illnesses are formed in childhood through the reactions of parents and other significant adults and cannot be separated from the network of interpersonal relations. Children who are given love, respect, and approval, Sullivan claimed, grow up to be healthy adults, assured that they are worthy of love and esteem. Sullivan sought to emphasize the role of psychology as a preventative medicine by shifting its focus to the causes and fostering of mental health, instead of illness.

Kierkegaard, May, and existential psychology. Søren Kierkegaard (1813–1855) and Rollo May (1909–) achieved notoriety through their advocacy of a psychological approach whose roots lie in the European philosophy of existentialism. This doctrine says we feel at once infinitely great because we are part of universal systems and infinitely small and helpless because we must separate from those systems and die. Perceiving this "absurd" contradiction at the center of life leads to fear and anxiety; mental illness begins when we give in to this fear and fail to join ourselves permanently to larger systems by fulfilling our potential. Rather than analyzing past or current behavior, the prime concern of existentialist therapy is moving the client past alienation and despair, to the realization of one's possibilities and the sense of a meaningful life.

R. D. Laing and liberation therapy. R. D. Laing (1927–1989) felt the mind, like the body, has its own natural healing mechanisms, and that mental illness isn't an "illness" at all but the mind's attempt to heal the wounds inflicted by an insane society. In his view, it was not women and men who are crazy but the world around them. Given support and asylum from the "slings and arrows" of the maddened world, their condition will resolve itself in greater sanity and emotional stability. Laing opposed medication for even the most severe mental illnesses, believing any medicine or therapy aimed at adjusting the individual to society disrupted the healing process and forced clients into a toxic, dysfunctional world that would only wound them.

Abraham Maslow and humanistic psychology. Abraham Maslow (1908–1970) concentrated on seeking the causes of mental health instead of illness. He studied women and men leading productive, fulfilling lives instead of the troubled and confused. Maslow viewed our basic drive as the need to grow and fulfill our lives in satisfying, positive ways (self-actualization). Mental illness begins when parents force children to choose between the love and pursuits vital to the child's fulfillment, or when they are robbed of self-esteem and given a negative image of their talents and character. Humanistic psychology aims at helping us remove these barriers to self-actualization. When we unconsciously say something during therapy that provides clues to the heart of our problems, the therapist repeats it, directing our attention to beliefs and feelings blocking our path to health.

Carl Rogers and client-centered therapy. Carl Rogers (1902–1987) believed the capacity for change and resolving problems is already within us and the function of the therapist is to support and encourage these positive, healthy impulses. Each of us, as an infant, learns what is self-actualizing and what is not; mental illness begins when what is self-actualizing for us is not met with a positive response by people in our environment. Through unqualified positive regard, the therapist encourages us to choose those experiences that enhance our self-actualization.

Eric Berne and transactional analysis. Eric Berne (1910–1970) revolted against psychology's technical language, lengthiness, and failure to offer concrete solutions to the problems women and men brought to therapy. Berne's simplified system was easy to lampoon, but its effectiveness soon made it a major influence in late twentieth-century psychology:

> · **Our three-part personality**. The Parent, the criticisms and warnings we internalized from our parents. The Adult, our reasoning, mediating self. The Child, our playful, carefree self.
> · **Transactions**. Exchanges that take place between two people—one or more of our three personalities takes part in each transaction.
> · **Scripts**. Our own plans for our life, and the people and events in it—frequently not consciously thought out and influenced by childhood experiences

Mental illness results when all we've learned are self-destructive scripts, or when our personality is dominated by the critical parent or the irresponsible child or bounces back and forth between the two. The goal of transactional analysis is to help us avoid self-destructive scripts, moving from playing games to intimacy by learning how to reassure our parent, support our child, and build a strong adult state of being.

Arthur Janov and primal therapy. Arthur Janov (1924–) believed that as infants we often experience an immediate need for love and the primal agony of not having it met. By the time we reach adulthood, this pain has long been covered over and buried in the unconscious, leaving us with an inexplicable feeling of anger and loss. This primal pain can only be released through reconnecting with it, reexperiencing it, and releasing it—through violent physical activity or the famous "primal scream."

Gestalt therapy. Max Wertheimer (1880–1943) Inspired by the German word *Gestalten*, "parts working together as a whole," this school believes psychology can never understand the mind by studying its components and should instead consider the whole. It emphasizes the unity of individuals and groups. Mental illness begins in childhood when the unity of the self (thought, feelings, action) is split, and we are forced to suppress important aspects of our personality, overemphasize others. One result is faulty communication between the parts of the self as well as the world around it. Gestalt therapists can be confrontational, encouraging our movement toward wholeness by abrasively challenging the defenses that keep us from facing our disenfranchised selves.

J. L. Moreno and psychodrama. J. L. Moreno (1892–1958) founded psychodrama which produces insights and resolves damaging feelings by having us reenact, with the aid of others, important scenes from our lives. Psychodrama allows us to safely experience and reexamine the feelings these scenes generate under the guidance of a therapist. By confronting an overcritical mother in the psychodrama, for example, we may make key discoveries about our relationship with her; by reversing roles with the person playing our mother, we may begin to see things from our mother's point of view. During psychodrama men and women often experience intense emotional release, breaking into tears or screaming at the participant playing a relative.

Today, psychology continues to spread and diverge into a multitude of forms, isms, and therapies. Each, perhaps, lays claim to a larger share of "truth" and a higher "cure" rate than the others. But all this is only the healthy ferment of a young and growing discipline.

SOURCE: McWhirter and McWhirter, *Illustrated Encyclopedia*; Robson and Edwards, *Getting Help*.

Putting the Body to Work

Since the body affects the mind (and vice versa), some therapies aim at working the kinks out of our minds by working them out of our bodies. Professionals have dubbed these "new" therapeutic approaches "bodywork." There are dozens of different kinds of bodywork, but all fall into one of four traditions:

The energetic tradition. The oldest of the four is based on the ancient belief that divine, cosmic, or universal energy can flow through the hands of a healer to an ailing person, strengthening her or him and speeding recovery. The most systematic presentations of this tradition are:

  · The chakras of Hindu mysticism.
  · The acupuncture meridians of Chinese medicine.

The mechanical tradition. Unlike the others, this tradition concerns itself solely with the physical relief of bodily stresses. It says we live fundamentally through our bodies, and that emotional, mental, and spiritual health depend on the body's ability to function well. It views the body only as an interrelated system of pulleys, levers, hinges, and plates that can become worn or misaligned because of stress and tension. The most celebrated schools of the mechanical tradition include:

- Rolfing.
- The Seever method.
- The Trager system.
- Alexander technique.
- Feldenkras method.
- Chiropractic & osteopathy.

The psychological tradition. Believes emotional health can be achieved only when our energy (emotional and muscular) can flow freely through the body. Mental illness is created when we tense up against the pains and betrayals of childhood and block the flow of this energy. This tradition seeks to release this tension directly by physical manipulation and pressure on the muscles and nerve pathways. The psychological tradition was pioneered by:

- Reichian therapy.
- Bioenergetics.

The integrative tradition. Views body and mind as a complex, interactive system and attempts to free the energies locked in both by unifying the first three traditions (energetic, mechanical, and psychological) with common elements in meditation, exercise, yoga, and the martial arts. The leading movement in the integrative tradition is:

- Hellerwork.

Warning: According to the theories on which bodywork is based, when the body (especially, in childhood), tenses up to lock out an unpleasant experience, it locks in the memories and emotions associated with that event. Deeply buried emotions and memories—often involving fear, grief, humiliation—can be released by these therapies. However, licensed bodyworkers are trained to help channel and release any negative emotions that surface in a positive way.

SOURCE: Murphy, *Future of the Body*; Heller and Henkin, *Bodywise*.

Problems and Patients

THERAPISTS WHO'S WHO

You Can't Tell Them Apart Without a Program

Psychiatrists, psychologists, and psychotherapists—what's the difference? It's subtle but vital. Most people can't tell the players apart without a program:

Psychiatrists. The elite among therapists, psychiatrists are M.D.s, physicians who specialize in treating mental disorders and illnesses. They are the only mental health professionals allowed to prescribe drugs and medicines.

Psychologists. Therapists with M.A.s or Ph.D.s, trained to help mentally healthy people or those with less serious mental disorders gain the insights and personal skills needed to successfully navigate difficult life crises or to reverse self-defeating behaviors.

Marriage counselors. Therapists, often psychologists, specializing in helping men and women find more effective ways to cope with troublesome family interactions.

All are "psychotherapists" (although some psychiatrists would strongly disagree). Roughly 50 percent have undergone personal psychotherapy themselves.

SOURCE: Maxmen, *New Psychiatry*.

Overanalyzed

There are 35,000 psychiatrists, 65,000 psychologists, and 150,000 other mental health workers in the United States. That's one therapist for every thousand people—a higher proportion of therapists than can be found in any other nation.

SOURCE: American Psychiatric Association, *Psychiatric Manpower*; Hoffman, *World Almanac*.

Are You a YAVIS?

Do therapists like some clients more than others? Psychotherapists try to remain objective, but they have their preferences just like everyone else, according to psychiatrist Jerrold Maxmen, M.D. He believes that clients with novel backgrounds, jobs, lifestyles, or experiences fascinate therapists. So do clients who make witty or insightful observations that would never have occurred to the therapist.

Although they fight it, therapists also tend to relate better to clients from backgrounds similar to their own. But what they like best of all, according to therapists Mandy Aftel and Robin Lakoff, are YAVISs (young, attractive, verbal, intelligent, and successful). YAVISs have more appealing, engaging personalities than most clients. So they are more often encouraged to enter therapy and to remain in therapy longer than others, say Aftel and Lakoff.

SOURCE: Aftel and Lakoff, *When Talk Is Not Cheap*; Maxmen, *New Psychiatry*.

What Kind of Person Becomes a Shrink?

Some think of psychotherapists as paragons of mental health, free of the self-defeating hang-ups that beset the rest of us. Others believe that only those with psychological problems of their own are attracted to the ranks of the profession, seeking to cure themselves as they cure their clients. A national survey of postgraduate students planning on careers as therapists found some truth on both sides, according to physician Donald Light, M. D.

There was plenty of evidence that those who become therapists are more nurturing, feel at ease with greater degrees of intimacy, and are more independent than most women and men. Test results showed they relate better to unstructured time and ambiguous situations, and are more reluctant to control other people's behavior. They are also less concerned about power and status, and more open about their feelings.

But there was also evidence that some potential therapists can bring strong psychological problems along with them into the profession. Though brighter and more verbal than other students, their academic achievements were actually poorer than average. The budding young students surveyed also reported greater dissatisfaction, lower self-esteem, greater anxiety, deeper cynicism, and significantly more serious worries about death than others.

Conclusion: When looking for a therapist, your best bet seems to be to pick one who's seeing a shrink.

SOURCE: Light, *Becoming a Psychiatrist.*

The Blame Game

Therapists always advise clients to stop blaming others and take responsibility for their own problems when things go wrong. But when therapy proves unsuccessful, says psychotherapy critic Hans Strupp, M.D., therapists minimize their own contribution to the process, and instead blame the client. They explain their failure to colleagues with phrases like, The client wasn't sufficiently motivated, or, The client was afraid to change. This therapeutic "blame game" outrages Strupp, who says the client has already proved his or her motivation by seeking help. If men and women lose the desire to make progress, Strupp claims, it is because their therapists failed to motivate them.

SOURCE: Strupp, *Psychotherapy for Better or Worse.*

It's the Vogue

When a new illness is discovered—or an old one is the subject of a major new study—the number of cases therapists diagnose increases dramatically. Psychologists call this "diagnostic vogue bias."

Researching case histories at Boston's McLean Hospital, a team of psychologists found the number of patients diagnosed with a disease increased with the number of publications written about it. Anxiety and phobias were the rage at the turn of the century. Then schizophrenia became the most diagnosed disease; later manic depression had its turn. Today obsessive-compulsive disorders (addiction) rank number one.

SOURCE: "Disorder of the Day," *Psychology Today*, June 1989.

How Therapists Feel About Clients

How can therapists listen to all the lurid, dramatic revelations their clients make and still remain objective, dispassionate observers? Don't they ever react to the secrets they are told and the emotional anguish they see? Therapists have trained themselves to appear dispassionate and supportive, according to psychiatrist Jerrold Maxmen, M.D. But underneath their carefully cultivated exteriors, they are often deeply affected by what they hear. "Psychiatrists are moved, shocked, amazed, disgusted, thrilled, disappointed, enchanted, and everything else by patients," Maxmen says.

SOURCE: Maxmen, *New Psychiatry*.

Why Therapy Goes Wrong

When therapy fails, the therapist is usually at fault, according to a survey of 70 leading psychotherapists. The survey, conducted by psychiatrist Hans Strupp, Ph.D., found that the therapeutic process may go wrong because therapists:

- Promised more than they could deliver.
- Lacked respect for their clients.
- Misdiagnosed their clients.
- Had excessive psychological problems of their own (especially hostility and seductiveness toward clients).
- Failed to convey enough hope to their clients.

SOURCE: Strupp, Hadley, and Gomes-Schwartz, *Psychotherapy for Better or Worse.*

Therapists Pick the Top 10 Self-Help Books

"Bibliotherapy" is the term therapists use for help we receive from reading books that offer insight into our personal problems. More than 65 percent of the psychotherapists polled in a study told interviewers they feel self-help books have an important place in the therapeutic process and encourage clients to read them. However, while therapists considered these books a helpful adjunct to therapy, they did not consider them a substitute. The 10 books therapists recommended most often were:

1. *The Relaxation Response* by Herbert Benson and Miriam Z. Klipped.
2. *On Death and Dying* by Elisabeth Kübler-Ross.
3. *Parent Effectiveness Training* by Thomas Gordon.
4. *Between Parent and Child* by Haim G. Ginott.
5. *Your Perfect Right: A Guide to Assertive Living* by Robert Alberti and Michael Emmons.
6. *What Color Is Your Parachute?* by Richard N. Bolles.
7. *When I Say No I Feel Guilty* by Manuel Smith.
8. *The Boys and Girls Book about Divorce* by Richard A. Gardner.
9. *Feeling Good: The New Mood Therapy* by David D. Burns.
10. *How to Survive the Loss of a Love* by Melba Colgrove, Harold Bloomfield, and Peter McWilliams.

SOURCE: Maxmen, *New Psychiatry.*

Faking It

Sometimes people try to fake mental problems to get attention, escape work, or to avoid punishment. But they don't fool their therapist for very long. While therapists may be taken in at first, clients rarely succeed in deceiving them over any extended period of time. Eventually a therapist notices the client is "with it" or "out of it" depending on what's "convenient," and begins to suspect the patient may be faking his or her symptoms.

SOURCE: Ibid.

PATIENTS

Not a Patient Group

Contemporary therapists never call those they serve "patients." They feel the traditional doctor-patient relationship is a bad model for successful therapy, since it implies an authority figure who alone possesses the knowledge and the ability to "cure" an ignorant, dependent patient. "Client" suggests a relationship between equals, a client and a specialist he or she has hired to assist with achieving specific goals. The term is healthier because it implies the client is beleaguered by problems that can be solved rather than an illness to be cured.

SOURCE: Aftel and Lakoff, *When Talk Is Not Cheap.*

Losing Control

Many men and women entering therapy are haunted by the thought of stumbling into deep emotional waters, losing control, and looking foolish during their first session with a therapist. But clients rarely "freak out" during the initial interview, according to author Jerrold S. Maxmen, M.D. In surveys cited by Maxmen, clients typically refrained from discussing the kind of highly charged emotional issues that might cause them to "lose control" (i.e., tap deep feelings) until after they developed a strong bond of trust with a therapist. Often people who had spent weeks dreading an initial emotional catharsis reported disappointment when the first visit failed to produce one.

SOURCE: Maxmen, *New Psychiatry.*

If You Can't Trust Your Therapist, Who Can You Trust?

People who don't get anywhere in therapy may be blocking their own progress. When promised complete anonymity, almost half (42 percent) of the participants in a poll at one Texas clinic admitted concealing crucial thoughts and actions from their therapists. Women tended to be dishonest about sexual thoughts; males about anger and violence.

The Texas findings may explain why some of us seem to remain stuck in therapy "forever." Inability to cope with feelings about sex and violence underlies many psychological problems. Unless we can be honest about these aspects of our lives, it is difficult to benefit from therapy.

Considering what therapists charge, those who prolong the process by withholding the truth truly pay for their misdeeds.

SOURCE: Klinger, *Daydreaming.*

The Therapeutic Attitude

The right attitude can get you a long way in life, and in therapy, too. You need to possess a little native curiosity about how your own mind works and be willing to embrace personal change, according to therapist Jerrold Maxmen, M.D.

Most clients wonder if they're getting everything they can from therapy. Since therapy costs money, takes time, and involves the outcome of important personal issues, it's a legitimate concern, Maxmen acknowledges. Clients make the fastest and most enduring progress when they have the "therapeutic attitude." Curiosity about our own feelings, thoughts, and actions is one element of this attitude. A firm focus on how we can change ourselves, rather than blaming our problems on others, is the other element.

SOURCE: Maxmen, *New Psychiatry*.

What Patients Want to Know About Therapists' Lives

Therapists constantly ask clients about their private lives. But one study reveals clients would like to do the asking for a change. Among the questions clients most wanted answered were:

- Are you married?
- If so, do you have children?
- What's your religion?
- Do you talk about me to your colleagues?
- Do you talk about me to your spouse?
- Do you think about me between our sessions?
- Do you ever dream about me?
- Do you like me?
- Am I your favorite client?
- If I were not your client, would you want me as a friend?

This curiosity probably represents a desire to see the human side of someone who seems well nigh omnipotent to many clients.

SOURCE: Ibid.

When Our Bodies Blab

We may think we are concealing our thoughts from our therapists, but the only person we're fooling is ourselves. According to Jerrold Maxmen, M.D., every movement we make, including many we are unaware of, telegraphs our actual thoughts and feelings straight to our therapists. When we suddenly shift position, the therapist immediately notes what we are talking about, since people often do this when they are discussing highly charged subjects. When we cross our arms, it's a good sign the current topic makes us feel defensive. Looking away from the therapist—especially up at the ceiling or down at the floor—is a strong indicator we are about to lie. And according to research reported in the *American Journal of Psychiatry*, whether our thighs carry our lower legs along when we walk, or our lower legs propel our thighs forward, can tell a therapist whether we are suffering from clinical depression.

SOURCE: Lawrence Sloman, "Gait Patterns of Depressed and Normal Patients," *American Journal of Psychiatry*, Vol. 139, 1982.

Getting to the Root of the Problem

According to therapist Jerrold Maxmen, M.D., clients who tell their therapists they want to get to the root of their problems have been misled by a popular myth: the belief that our emotional and personal troubles arise from a traumatic circumstance or incident in childhood. But for many of us, our psychological problems don't necessarily have a single root, according to Maxmen. Instead, there may be many roots twining from our genetic heritage, through our youth, to the impacts of adult life. The concept of the single root can be very harmful to some of those just entering therapy, says Maxmen. When these clients discover they won't be magically cured as soon as the therapist uproots some forgotten childhood trauma, they often drop out of the process. Our problems, Maxmen seems to suggest, are less like trees with a single root system than weeds that spring up throughout our mental garden.

SOURCE: Maxmen, *New Psychiatry*.

Picking a Therapist

If you reach the point in life where you find yourself seeking a therapist, how do you know when you've found a good one? Therapists Mandy Aftel and Robin Lakoff suggest women and men meeting a therapist for the first time ask themselves:

- Did the therapist seem to understand what you were trying to say?
- Was the therapist someone you felt you could trust?
- Did the therapist listen to your position when you felt misunderstood?
- Did you feel comfortable enough with the therapist to be honest and direct?
- Did the therapist maintain eye contact?
- Did you feel the therapist was interested in you (and not preoccupied with other things)?
- Did you feel the therapist gave you adequate feedback?
- Did the therapist make a direct statement about wanting to work with you?
- Did the therapist make any rules clear at the outset?
- Did the therapist set you at ease about asking any questions you had?

If you can answer "yes" to most of these, you may have found the kind of caring, responsible therapist every client dreams about.

SOURCE: Aftel and Lakoff, *When Talk Is Not Cheap.*

ILLNESSES

You Don't Have to Be Crazy . . .

"You have to be crazy to see a therapist," according to one old joke. But the vast majority (80 percent) of those involved in psychotherapy aren't "crazy" at all. They only lack skills for coping with everyday problems of living—depression following personal loss, confusion over relationships, value conflicts, anger, indecisiveness, etc.

Many of the rest have what therapists consider minor mental disorders—phobias, anxiety, and panic attacks, for example—exaggerations of "normal" behavior (which may be heightened by slight imbalances in brain chemistry in rare instances) that are more troublesome to the victims than to those around them. A small percentage have serious mental illnesses (resulting from significant chemical imbalances)—schizophrenia, major depression, manic depression—that impair their ability to function in the "real" world.

Only a fraction, around 1 percent, are "crazy." Therapists, writes Jerrold Maxmen, M.D., reserve this term exclusively for "psychotics," "people who have lost touch with reality" and are themselves lost, in a world of hallucination and delusion.

SOURCE: Maxmen, *New Psychiatry*.

210 Ways to Lose Your Mind

Less than 20 percent of us suffer actual mental disorders, but those who do suffer from an amazing variety of afflictions. The *Diagnostic and Statistical Manual of Mental Disorders*, the therapist's bible, lists 210 separate illnesses, and literally thousands of secondary syndromes. Among the best-known are bipolar disorder (manic depression), dysthymic disorder (depression), obsessive-compulsive disorder, and schizophrenia. Among the rest are such arcane diseases such as: schizo-hystero iddysphoria, seasonal affective disorder, anosognosia, neuroleptic malignant syndrome, attention-deficit disorder, Munchausen's syndrome, and hypomanic state-hebephrenic schizo-depersonalization.

SOURCE: Ibid.

Permanent Guests

While one out of five of us suffer from what therapists define as a mental disorder only 2 percent of us have extreme mental illnesses—but however small, the number is still too large. In the United States alone, that totals 5 million people.

Each year about 500,000 women and men are briefly hospitalized due to emotional or psychological problems—

accounting for almost half of all hospital patients. Another 2 million receive treatment as outpatients. But the only treatment the remaining 2.5 million receive is life on the streets.

SOURCE: Zilbergeld, *Shrinking of America*; Hoffman, *World Almanac*.

The Dope About Disorders

Most of us know less about mental illness than we do about the dark side of the moon. Asked to name five, we'd be lucky to get two right. Asked to describe their symptoms, we'd probably find ourselves at a loss for words. Below is the lowdown on the illnesses you're most likely to be hearing more about.

Affective disorders. Involve disturbances of mood; victims are too "up" (manic), too "down" (major depression, a leading cause of suicide), or alternate between the two (manic depression).

Anxiety disorders. Chronic, acute unease, anxiety, and fear; includes phobias (irrational fears of people, places, and things) and panic disorders (paralyzing attacks of anxiety or fear triggered by specific situations).

Obsessive-compulsive and addictive disorders. Uncontrollable, irrational, and self-destructive behaviors:

· **Obsessive thoughts** that dominate the victim's behavior.
· **Compulsive actions:** A repetitive behavior the victim is unable to restrain.
· **Addiction:** Obsessive-compulsive abuse of substances, credit, sex, religion, and just about anything else.

Personality disorders. Victims appear intelligent and personable on the outside, but inside they are morally empty, calculating, and cruel.

Schizophrenia. The ability to think and talk in a consistently clear, logical, and rational manner is seriously disrupted; can come and go for hours, days, weeks, months, or even years at a time. Among its most identifiable symptoms are:

· **Delusions:** Obviously false beliefs that tend toward the bizarre.
· **Disturbed thinking:** Thoughts bounce from topic to topic with no apparent rhyme or reason.

Unfortunately, with budget cutbacks, fewer and fewer of the men and women affected with these illnesses receive any treatment at all.

SOURCE: Woolis, *When Someone You Love*; Nelson, *Healing the Split*.

Dope for Disorders

What causes mental illness? A visitation from the gods and punishment for sin were humans' first guesses. Then Freud found evidence linking emotional difficulties to traumatic events and unhealthy family interactions during childhood. Next, psychologists discovered strong connections to faulty thinking patterns that could easily be relearned. Biological causes became the next suspect, as science began studying the mind's physiology. Genetic studies established that many mental illnesses run in families, while abnormalities in brain structure were thought to explain others.

The newest suspect is brain chemistry: the messenger molecules that carry signals across the gap between brain cells, according to psychiatrist Jerrold Maxmen, M.D. Four brain chemicals seem to play key roles in the creation of mental disorders: (1) dopamine—excessive levels appear to trigger schizophrenia, (2) norepinephrine—increases seem to trigger mania, while decreases trigger depression, (3) serotonin—fluctuations appear to trigger sleep and mood disorders, and (4) agmma-aminobutyric acid—lowered levels are associated with anxiety and panic disorders. Strong substantiation for the chemical theory of mental illness comes from the fact that when patients take the drugs needed to correct these imbalances, symptoms lessen or vanish.

Other psychotherapists acknowledge that brain chemistry plays an important role, but point to mountains of evidence linking mental illness to psychological causes. The question of whether alterations in brain chemistry cause mental illness or result from it, they say, has yet to be answered.

Experiments reported in *The 3-Pound Universe* seem to unite these seemingly divergent theories. Men and women who had normal brain chemistries before the loss of a loved one showed decreased levels of norepinephrine during the depression that followed; but in patients subject to clinical depression, norepinephrine levels suddenly lowered without an emotional cause, triggering an attack. Apparently mental disturbance can trigger chemical shifts in the brain, but chemical shifts can also trigger mental illness.

SOURCE: Hooper and Teresi, *3-Pound Universe*; Maxmen, *New Psychiatry*.

Crazy About Madness

Certain diseases, such as cancer, strike such dread into our hearts, we don't even want to think about them. One of these is mental illness in any kind or degree. In some of us, the fear of mental illness becomes a mental illness itself. We never mention the subject, change the topic hastily when it's introduced, cross the street to avoid those who act mentally ill, drop friends suspected of having psychological problems, and worry constantly that we or others might be "going crazy." Psychologists have a name for this condition: lyssophobia, the fear of insanity.

SOURCE: McWhirter and McWhirter, *Illustrated Encyclopedia*.

Munchausen's Syndrome

Some people suffer from a compulsion to fake serious illnesses and be hospitalized. Therapists call this condition "Munchausen's syndrome" naming it after the legendary eighteenth-century Baron

Munchausen, famed for the wildly exaggerated lies he told about himself. Psychiatrist Bernard Schwartz believes Munchausen patients find their lives intolerable and hunger for the attention, care, and isolation from outside problems that accompany hospitalization.

Though it sounds harmless, Munchausen's syndrome can be a life-threatening disorder. Victims will do anything to enter and remain in hospitals: injure themselves, drink toxic substances, and trick physicians into unnecessary surgery, over and over again. Even when caught red-handed, Munchausen patients refuse to acknowledge they faked symptoms. They simply disappear and start all over with a new doctor and a whole new set of symptoms.

SOURCE: Schwartz, *When the Body.*

How Does It Feel?

What does it feel like to be mentally ill? According to psychologist Rebecca Woolis, Ph.D., fear is the dominating emotion. Schizophrenia, manic depression, and panic attacks can strike without warning. The sufferer lives in constant dread of each new occurrence. Ordinary events take on an exaggerated importance: Other people's words and actions, the weather, even a routine traffic accident, can seem to be divine messages or part of a conspiracy directed against you. Other people are maddeningly unable to understand what you are saying, and you have trouble making sense of them. Worse, when you do understand what they say much of it seems hostile and negative. More frightening still, you lack the energy to resist both a world that is overwhelmingly threatening and the uncontrollable forces working inside you.

SOURCE: Woolis, *When Someone You Love.*

Brain Damage

Brain damage, the subject of a million tasteless jokes, is no laughing matter. Damage to the brain causes many bizarre disorders, some relatively benign, others frightening, even devastating. Among them:

- aboulia (lack of will or initiative)
- agrypnia (total inability to sleep)
- alexia (inability to understand the printed word)
- algolagnia (lust for pain)
- amimia (loss of expressive capabilities)
- amorphia (inability to judge form)
- aphagia (inability to swallow)
- bradykinesia (slowness of movement)
- catalepsy (rigidity of posture)
- choreas (involuntary "flickering" muscle movements)
- echolalia (parroting of words)
- echopraxia (parroting of actions)
- ophthalmoplegia (paralysis of gaze)
- orexia (incontinent gluttony)
- tachykinesia (excessive speed of movement).

SOURCE: Hooper and Teresi, *3-Pound Universe.*

The Thirteenth Step

In the 1980s the world went on a recovery binge. By decade's end *Newsweek* reported more than 500,000 12-step type groups (based upon Alcoholics Anonymous's 12 steps of recovery) had sprung up nationwide, helping members manage dozens of addictions including relationships, gambling, sex, drugs, spending, and a host of others.

Clearly, 12-step groups have helped millions of alcoholics and addicts. Before the advent of Alcoholics Anonymous, addiction recovery rates were nonexistent and permanent cure was believed impossible. These groups have also enabled millions to successfully manage many other self-destructive behaviors.

But recovery groups also have what psychologist Stanton Peele calls their "dark side." Some therapists began to talk of America's addiction to recovery and recovery from recovery. Critics such as Peele brand 12-step programs "a kind of brainwashing," a developmental dead end that denies members future growth and progress. Participants are told "recovery is forever," they will "always" be addicts, and will always need to "keep coming back." For some members this seems to reinforce the dependency that brought them to the group, leading them to become as dependent on it as they ever were on alcohol or drugs. Such members attend meetings 1, 5, even 14 times or more per week. Some of those who receive benefit from one program discover yet other addictions that can benefit from a 12-step approach.

SOURCE: Tessina, *The Thirteenth Step*.

ABERRATIONS

Winter Blues

The sun's rays keep us happy. When daylight shortens in winter, melancholy settles over many men and women. Psychologists call this seasonal affective order (SAD). The changing season was once blamed. However, sunlight, not the unconscious, may be responsible for winter blues.

Research conducted by Alfred Levy, M.D., at Portland's Oregon Health Sciences University is shedding new light on the subject. Levy knew that melatonin, a key mood elevator, is produced by sunlight. Since there is less light in winter, he wondered if lowered melatonin levels might trigger SAD.

Levy had sufferers bask under bright artificial sunlight for at least half an hour every morning. The majority soon lost their winter blues. Prolonged exposure to real sunlight, Levy claims, would have a similar curative effect. Levy's findings may explain the attraction of tropical vacations during the winter months.

SOURCE: Alfred J. Levy, "Seasonal Affective Disorder," *Science*, Vol. 2325, 1987.

Just Don't Breathe

Traditionally, good samaritans tell victims of panic to take a deep breath and relax (or slap them sharply on the face). They believe that increased oxygen has a calming effect on the body. But taking a deep breath may be the worst thing panic sufferers can do, according to David V. Sheehan, director of clinical research at the University of South Florida.

Because some drugs relieve or prevent panic attacks, Sheehan believed the condition might have biological roots. Soon he discovered even modestly increased traces of carbon dioxide in the atmosphere can trigger panic in many sufferers. Breathing deeply means inhaling more carbon dioxide, making the attack worse, not better. Panic, Sheehan's research suggests, is no slapping matter.

SOURCE: David Sheehan and Scott M. Fishman, "Don't Panic," *Psychology Today*, April 1988.

The Incredible Shrinking Penis

Most men worry about the size of their penis; some even worry that it might shrink. But a handful of males suffer from a psychological syndrome called "koro": an overwhelming fear that their penis is shrinking into the belly. Koro strikes during periods of increased stress due to holidays, work and relationship problems, and important events. First identified in the Far East, the syndrome's most extreme form includes the conviction that when the penis finishes contracting into the belly, the victim will die.

A team of British researchers devised a way to reassure males afflicted with this obsession. Using the "penal plethysmograph," which detects changes in circumference, they convinced sufferers their manhood showed no decrease in size. Ironically, the British team discovered that, while the victim's organs were not shrinking, attacks of koro caused temporary contraction.

SOURCE: Laurence Miller, "The Incredible Shrinking . . . ," *Psychology Today*, July 1986.

Compulsive Liars

Everyone lies sometimes—usually to escape a sticky situation. But some of us lie all the time. In fact, one out of every 20 people we meet is a compulsive liar, according to Bryan King, a psychiatrist at the UCLA School of Medicine.

Compulsive liars are simply unable to tell the truth. Unlike the rest of us, who only lie when we think we have to, compulsive liars fabulate for the sake of fabulation. King, who has studied lying for years, believes compulsive liars come from traumatic home environments. Their own history is so bad, they revise it.

The feeling of liberation from a past they can't face becomes addictive, giving compulsive liars motivation to stretch the truth again and again. "They get an instant rush by duping someone," according to psychiatry professor Charles Ford.

Both men view compulsive lying as an emotional illness. Victims don't just tell lies, they try to live them. When compulsive liars start to believe their revised versions, a whole new fictionalized world opens up for them, according to Ford. Until caught, they experience a new self-esteem, a new sense of power.

Compulsive liars are difficult to help, because the success of therapy depends in large part upon the one quality that most of them lack: honesty.

SOURCE: Gordon Monson, "The One That Got Away and Other Tall Tales," *Los Angeles Times*, February 7, 1990.

A Hairy Problem

People who are angry or frustrated often jokingly threaten to pull their hair out. But for some people hair-pulling is no joke—they have a hair fetish known as "trichotillomania." Researchers have linked stress to more than 25 percent of trichotillomania cases. Victims appear "wigged out" by stress.

SOURCE: "Personal Q&A," *Psychology Today*, January/February 1989.

PHOBIAS

Not a Case of Logophobia

We all have some kind of irrational fear (phobia)—bees, dogs, elevators, dentists, the dark. People can develop phobias about anything: a person, place, thing, idea, group, or situation. Some of us have one phobia (monophobia); some have many (polyphobia); others are fearful of everything (panphobia). More than 170 phobias have been identified. Some of them common and understandable, others bizarre and unlikely.

Our more common phobias are:

- agoraphobia (open spaces)
- algophobia (pain)
- ailurophobia (cats)
- arachnophobia (spiders)
- apiphobia (bees)
- cynophobia (dogs)
- aviophobia (flying)
- xenophobia (foreigners)
- astraphobia (storms)
- zoophobia (animals)
- iatrophobia (doctors)
- acrophobia (heights)

Our less common, but more understandable, phobias include:

- ballistophobia (bullets)
- thasophobia (sitting idle)
- harpaxophobia (robbers)
- astraphobia (lightning)
- hypegiaphobia (responsibility)
- taphephobia (being buried alive)
- phasmophobia (ghosts)
- thalassophobia (the ocean)

Among our more bizarre, if harmless, phobias are:

- trichophobia (hair)
- kyphophobia (stooping)
- aulophobia (flutes)
- linonophobia (string)
- dendrophobia (trees)
- patroiophobia (heredity)

- pteronophobia (feathers)
- siderophobia (stars)
- odontophobia (teeth)
- belonephobia (needles)

- ombrophobia (rain)
- amathophobia (dust)
- crystallophobia (crystals)

But a few phobias can be very inconvenient:

- oophobia (opening one's eyes)
- sistophobia (food)
- vestiphobia (clothing)
- dermatophobia (skin)
- hypnophobia (sleep)
- phagophobia (swallowing)

- ochophobia (vehicles)
- gephydrophobia (crossing bridges)
- nyctophobia (night)
- oikophobia (home)
- clinophobia (beds)

A few are even philosophic:

- eleuthrophobia (freedom)
- neophobia (the new)
- ergophobia (work)
- ideophobia (ideas)
- mechanophobia (machinery)
- dikephobia (justice)
- kakorraphiaphobia (failure)
- gymnophobia (nudity)
- bibliophobia (books)

- hednophobia (pleasure)
- peccatophobia (sinning)
- satanophobia (Satan)
- androphobia (men)
- gynophobia (women)
- anthropophobia (human beings)
- genophobia (sex)
- gametophobia (marriage)

Evidently, whatever else early twentieth-century therapists suffered from, they did not suffer from logophobia (fear of words) or phobophobia (fear of fears).

SOURCE: McWhirter and McWhirter, *Illustrated Encyclopedia.*

Fear of Fillings

No one likes going to the dentist. But for some people, fear of dentists is so overpowering it endangers their lives. Almost 15 percent of us put off making dental appointments until serious damage has occurred to our teeth, according to the Academy of General Dentistry. When treatment is unduly delayed, gum disease, tooth loss, internal infection, and a serious threat to life and health can result.

SOURCE: Susan Chollar, "Fear of Fillings," *Psychology Today*, January/February 1989.

Fear of Flying

No matter how often we hear statistics proving plane travel is safer than driving a car, we don't really believe it. The memory of highly publicized airplane disasters comes back to haunt us. That's because airplane crashes involve the deaths of hundreds of people and generate lurid headlines, while the garden variety auto fatality rarely rates more than a paragraph somewhere on page eight. As a result, according to magazine writer Carole Wade Offir, it's easy to recall the few airplane disasters we've heard about—and hard to recall the far greater number of accidents involving automobiles.

SOURCE: Carole Wade Offir, "Seven Quick Ways to Kid Yourself," *Glamour*, December 1992.

Our Psychological Development Over a Lifetime

CHILDHOOD

Never Too Young to Learn

Scientists long ago proved the truth of the axiom: You're never too old to learn. Now they have unearthed evidence that we're never too young to learn.

In one Brown University study, infants only two to four days old learned which sound, a tone or a buzzer, produced a taste of sugar water. In one other university study, newborns as young as 42 *minutes* learned to imitate facial gestures like sticking out the tongue. Parents who read the classics to infants and play them great music, convinced the influence will carry over into later life, may be on the right track after all.

SOURCE: Robert J. Trotter, "You've Come a Long Way, Baby," *Psychology Today*, May 1987.

Don't Blame Your Mom

Chronic anger, addiction, violence, failure, broken relationships, and many other adult problems have been traced to poor infant-mother bonding. But what prevents mothers and their babies from forming a warm emotional bond in the first place? For years psychologists believed babies developed personalities and preferences over a period of months, so whatever went wrong with the initial bonding process must be due to the mother.

A University of Delaware study suggests that many times moms are not to blame. Some infants are born with negative attitudes and personalities that prevent bonding—no matter how much love, care, or nurturing mothers shower on them. Fussy babies—those who demanded the most attention and became most anxious during stressful situations—were the most likely to bond poorly. Rather than reflecting a failure on their mother's part, these babies' inability to form a warm attachment with their moms reflected innate emotional and personality problems they would carry with them into adulthood.

SOURCE: Daniel Q. Haney, "Mother off the Hook on Bond with Baby," *Los Angeles Times*, April 1, 1990.

The Age of Reason

What's the age of reason? Two? Five? Thirty-five? When do we gain the ability to connect two events and reason from them? Some people never seem to develop it. But for most of us the age of reason is about one month after birth, claims psychologist Elizabeth S. Spelke.

Aware that babies stare longer at the new and novel than at the familiar and routine, Spelke decided to test the age at which babies first begin to reason. Infants between one and two months of age watched a rolling ball disappear behind a screen and the screen was removed, revealing it resting against a wall. Another group this age watched the ball disappear without being shown what caused it to stop. Babies shown what stopped the ball became bored more quickly watching the ball disappear, indicating they had connected the obstacle with the disappearance. Spelke believes her experiments prove that infants reason in basic ways about what they see.

Spelke's findings fly in the face of older scientific views on the brain structure of newborns: that the neurological connections necessary for reason don't develop for many months. If confirmed by others, her studies show there's reason to give new thought to how babies think.

SOURCE: Bruce Bower "Infants Signal the Birth of Knowledge," *Science News*, November 14, 1992.

The Thrill of the New

The secret of creating smarter babies may now be at parents' fingertips. Psychologist Marc H. Bornstein discovered that the more often mothers encouraged babies to look at new objects by pointing them out, the higher their offspring scored on intelligence tests later in life. Apparently the thrill of the new boosts babies' brain power.

SOURCE: John Rubin, "Boosting Baby's Brain," *Psychology Today*, March 1986.

The Dawn of the Self

When do we first become ourselves? At what point do we pass from the passive oblivion of infancy to the self-awareness of childhood? To find out, a team of Rutgers Medical School psychologists dabbed a spot of rouge on babies' noses and sat them in front of a mirror. Infants who touched their own nose rather than the mirror, the researchers reasoned, were obviously aware of themselves as separate and distinct entities. From the babies' responses, the Rutgers team fixed our dawning awareness of ourselves as separate from the world around us at between 18 and 24 months.

SOURCE: Wray Herbert, "A Sense of Self," *Psychology Today*, June 1986.

Babies Forgetting Birth

Why can't most of us recall anything that happened before we were three or four?

Those memories aren't lost—we're just looking for them in the wrong file drawer, says psychologist Neisser of Emory University. Adult recollections are linked to words, while an infant's memories are associated with visual and sensory cues. As a result, when we mentally flip through memories filed under Birthday Parties, we find only those from the age of four or five onward.

The "lost" recollections of infancy can be recovered, says Neisser. But only if we look for them where they are filed: with our sensory, rather than verbal memories. One of Neisser's students was kneeling down to install a gumball machine at his fraternity— and thus viewing the world from the height of a two-year-old— which triggered an onrush of childhood memories.

SOURCE: "Stages of Life, Ages of Mind," *Newsweek*, September 29, 1986.

The Birth of the Blues

Anger and happiness are the most basic emotions (even animals have them) and the first we develop as infants. The more complex emotions—the ones that make us human—develop later, around the age of two. At this point, we become aware of others as separate individuals and of our interactions with them. This leads to our first experiences of empathy, jealousy, shame, guilt, and pride, according to researchers at the Robert Wood Johnson Medical School. When this happens, babies become subject to depression and loneliness; unknowingly, they have just experienced the birth of the blues.

SOURCE: Robert J. Trotter, "You've Come a Long Way, Baby," *Psychology Today*, May 1987.

"I Don't Feel Good Today, Mommy!"

As children, we all tried to dodge grade school by pretending to be sick. Epidemics of sniffles, aches, pains, and other nonspecific complaints sweep the six to twelve age group routinely when class projects are due or on the day of important tests. Playing sick is a healthy part of childhood, according to the American Academy of Child and Adolescent Psychiatry.

But for some grade-schoolers, pretending to be sick is more than a sometime thing. Up to 10 percent of children "play sick" because of a deeper underlying anxiety. Therapists call this "school anxiety," and it can be set off by many things: temporary fear of school, teacher change, academic stress, illness, divorce, the death of a relative, or worries about crime, bullies, and scapegoating. Usually children are more than eager to confess their concerns when observant parents become aware there is a problem.

SOURCE: "I Won't Go to School," *Parents*, September 1990.

Ahead of the Pack

Gifted children are ahead of their peers in intellectual development, and they also appear to be ahead in developing emotional problems, as well. Psychologist Richard Klene found that gifted children tend to develop most childhood fears about two years before other kids their age. Without understanding and support from the adults around them, most gifted children found this a painful, confusing process. When parents were aware of their offspring's advanced emotional development and gave them special support, gifted children had no more difficulty handling these transitions than anyone else.

SOURCE: Paul Chance, "Precocious Fears in the Gifted," *Psychology Today*, April 1989.

The Critical Parent

No wonder so many of us grow up with shaky self-esteem. When it comes to verbal licks versus verbal strokes from parents, the picture we see painted of us is overwhelmingly negative. Parents criticize children five times for every compliment they bestow, according to psychologist Jane Marks. She suggests disbelieving parents keep track of how often they criticize and praise children for a few weeks.

Most parents are distressed at how far their licks outnumber strokes. But Marks offers quick reassurance: "Criticizing doesn't make you bad parents. It shows that you're trying to teach [your children]." She recommends complimenting specific behaviors so that children know exactly what the praise is for; she also cautions against confusing children by mixing praise and criticism at the same time.

SOURCE: Jane Marks, "We Have a Problem," *Parents*, September 1990.

Children Who Don't Play

Most of us envision childhood, especially the toddler years, as a time of carefree play. But some children don't play at all, writes psychologist Margaret Lowenfield. In a well-equipped nursery school, such a child will remain tense and refuse to play with any of the toys. Or he or she will aimlessly handle every toy without playing with any one and initiate half a dozen games, only to drop each moments later.

These children are suffering from an anxiety they can not describe. Because it is very difficult for young children to express what troubles them, they often retreat from the world. "Lack of ability to play is not natural and is not an inborn characteristic," Lowenfield warns. Children who don't play are sending a signal of a deeper underlying problem.

SOURCE: Lowenfield, *Children and Play*.

Bilingual or Split Personality?

Bilingual education has been highly touted. But now UCLA psychologists have unearthed disturbing evidence that being bilingual can produce a split personalitylike effect. Since these "coordinate bilinguals" learn their second language in a totally different culture, some researchers believe each language—and the national characteristics absorbed with them—may be stored in different parts of the brain. As a result, when coordinate bilinguals use a language, they unwittingly tap into the mannerisms and values that go with its culture.

A group of students from emerging nations who had learned English as a second language were given a personality assessment test, first in their native language and then, several weeks later, in English. Participants revealed notable personality differences depending on which language they used. While speaking English they scored higher in social presence, self-acceptance, well-being, and achievement, characteristic American values. When answering in their native tongue, they scored higher in self-control and the desire to create a good impression, qualities long valued in their native cultures.

Coordinate bilinguals, the researchers suggested, might be one personality pattern in their birth country, and a completely different personality in their adopted nation.

SOURCE: Cheryl Simon, "Dr. Jekyll, Señor Hyde," *Psychology Today*, December 1987.

ADOLESCENCE

Not a Kid Anymore

The psychological growth from childhood to adolescence is a gradual and largely invisible process. Even parents might not be able to pinpoint the difference between their childen and the teenagers they've become. But a University of Michigan study of changes in the way children and adolescents spend their day reveals clear differences and growth.

At the age of three, boys and girls typically sleep 10½ hours; but by age sixteen, they're down to 8 hours and 20 minutes, gaining more than 2 hours of waking time. Strangely, with this increase in waking time, television viewing actually declines among sixteen-year-olds to less than 2 hours, from a peak of 2½ at age ten, perhaps due to increasing preoccupation with the opposite gender. Play becomes a thing of the past, gone with childhood, down from 2 hours and 20 minutes to a mere 14 minutes. Time spent in personal grooming, not surprisingly, increases from 40 minutes in childhood to a full hour by midteens. Time spent with friends jumps from 10 minutes to nearly an hour.

SOURCE: Paul Chance and Joshua Fischman, "Magic of Childhood," *Psychology Today*, May 1987.

It's Not Rebellion

Teens can be very confusing to adults, and themselves: in turn angry, ecstatically happy, depressed, and ultramellow. Some of their highly combustible emotionality is due to the confusion and rebellion caused by moving into an adult world in which relationships and responsibilities are quite different. But many are triggered by the hormonal and central nervous system changes brought on by adolescence, according to researcher Ernest Lawrence Rossi, Ph.D. Teens are not being contrary purposely, says Rossi. Their shifting, volatile emotions more often reflect the hormonal shifts of puberty than adolescent rebellion.

SOURCE: Rossi, *Dreams and the Development of Personality*.

The Defiant Ones

Rebellion or defiance—what's the difference? It can be a very big difference where teenagers are concerned. Adolescent rebellion is one of life's most celebrated rites of passage. The vast majority of us shake it off and pass on to relatively normal adulthood. But for some young men and women, what appears to be adolescent rebellion is actually a more serious underlying disturbance therapists call "oppositional defiant disorder." Unchecked, this defiance grows worse, culminating in risk-taking behavior that can endanger the teen and others.

Oppositional defiant disorder can strike children as young as twelve or thirteen, writes Lee Salk, M.D., clinical professor of psychiatry and pediatrics at the Cornell Medical Center. Because troubled teens at first fit the same behavior patterns as other adolescents, parents often don't realize their offspring have a serious problem until an arrest, suicide attempt, automobile accident, or even criminal activity sends its own chilling signal. Normal adolescent rebellion, Salk says, is generally limited to the family circle. Only when defiance extends into other areas of life—school, friends, work—should parents become concerned. According to Salk, eight other telltale clues are:

- Frequent loss of temper.
- Frequent arguments with adults.
- Deliberately doing things that irritate others.
- Blaming others for one's own errors or mistakes.
- Being easily annoyed.
- Frequent anger and resentment.
- Frequent spitefulness and vindictiveness.
- Frequent swearing and using obscene language.

Fortunately, when these signals are detected early, therapy can help heal the causes of oppositional defiant disorder.

SOURCE: Lee Salk, "Adolescent Rebellion or Sheer Defiance?" *McCall's*, July 1990.

They're Either Too Young or Too Old

Pity the poor teenager. In a hurry to grow up, they now find themselves in a no-win situation, their bodies seeming to develop either too early or too late. When this happens, adolescents experience deep emotional anguish, suffering from their own insecurities and the taunts of their peers, according to James Comer, M.D., professor of child psychiatry at Yale University.

Girls whose bodies develop early (between eleven and thirteen) become the targets of sexual interest and pressure long before they are emotionally prepared for it. Grades and self-esteem can drop as a result. Boys who mature early also may experience a decline in grades and self-esteem. In regions where gang activity runs high, they are at serious risk of being pulled into gangs by older boys.

Boys and girls who mature late worry about their normality, frightened their bodies will never develop and that there is something "wrong with them." Girls see other girls becoming attractive to boys, while they remain ignored; boys find themselves the butt of ridicule, the last to be chosen in sports. Both typically find themselves frozen out of peer groups, Comer says.

Whether their bodies grow up too fast or too slow, nature seems to have played a cruel joke on these teens; and they need extra sensitivity and support to help ease them through this difficult transition.

SOURCE: James Comer, "Kids Who Mature Fast," *Parents*, June 1990.

The Grass Is Greener

Most teens envy their attractive peers, whom they perceive as assured, confident, and successful. But attractive teens are insecure about their looks and actually envy each other, according to surveys cited by researcher Gordian Patzer, Ph.D.

All adolescents are constantly worried about their appearance. To adults, this preoccupation may seem superficial and silly. But so many central aspects of adolescent life—friendship, social acceptance, sexual attractiveness—are determined by appearance that it's no wonder teens spend hours before the mirror examining themselves for flaws. Even the most attractive are more aware of their few deficiencies than the good features they possess.

SOURCE: David Elkind, "Teenagers Confront Mother Nature," *Parents*, May 1990.

Smarter Than You Think

Get set for a shock. Today's teens may have better values than their parents and grandparents. Asked to name who they would most like to date, readers of *Teen* chose athletes, cheerleaders, and students involved in drama and fine arts. Some members of earlier generations only yearned for athletes and cheerleaders, suggesting contemporary adolescents share intellectual interests their predecessors did not possess.

SOURCE: "Boy Baffled?" *Teen*, July 1990.

Brief Candles

One out of every 50,000 teenagers will take his or her own life this year. The death of the young—who have so much before them—is always a tragedy. A self-inflicted death is all the more wasteful. Yet teen suicides are becoming more common, affecting an entire generation of adolescents.

Over the last three decades, the number of teen suicides has tripled. More frighteningly, 30 percent of all adolescents admit they've seriously considered taking their own lives, while six out of every 100 have actually tried to kill themselves. This increase in teen suicide, writes child psychologist David Elkind, Ph.D., reflects the unprecedented challenges and perils contemporary adolescents face. Today's perils include sexual activity, drugs, and the divorce rate, for example. Worst of all, Elkind says, they are the first generation to have lost the sense that the world is getting better.

Teen suicides are usually triggered by a traumatic event: parents' divorce, breaking up with a boyfriend or girlfriend, or losing an important competition. But the cause is nearly always long-standing feelings of inadequacy, inferiority, persecution, or injustice. Any intimation that a teenager is contemplating suicide should always be taken seriously, Elkind warns. Teens who talk of taking their own lives are in a crisis. What they need most is a sympathetic listener who will not judge them. Often it is an enormous relief for adolescents to confess their self-destructive urges to someone else.

SOURCE: Elkind, *Hurried Child*.

The Fundamental Things Still Apply

How much has the love life of teenage boys and girls changed? Teens still struggle with the same old questions that plagued Andy Hardy and the ancient Egyptians. According to the results of a *Teen* report, the questions readers most wanted answered included:

- Where do you go to meet girls/guys?
- Who should pay for a date?
- Should girls ask guys out?
- What's the best way to let him/her know you're interested?
- Should a boy and girl date if she is taller than he is?
- If someone turns you down for a date, should you ever ask them out again?
- If you aren't interested in someone but they're still interested in you, what should you do?
- How should you go about breaking up with someone you've been seeing steadily?
- Should you go out with someone you know already has a boyfriend/girlfriend?

The French, who seem to have a saying to cover every aspect of *amour*, have one to cover the results of this survey, too: "The more things change, the more they stay the same."

SOURCE: "Baffled? 50 Answers to Your Questions," *Teen*, July 1990.

For Those Who Hate Young

Teen bigotry is on the rise, with intolerance and hate crimes growing among adolescents. According to a magazine survey, most of today's hatemongers are under the age of twenty-one.

Campuses have been reporting a 30 percent rise per year in hate crimes. In short, the boy (or girl) next door may be the bigot next door.

Why the rise in youthful bigotry? Psychologists name a variety of factors, among them: racial competition for diminishing job opportunities and college aid and lowered societal vigilance against bigotry following a period of long decline. But the most important factor may be that today's young people don't realize the appalling history of bigotry. "They don't know about gas chambers and lynchings," says Allan Ostar, president of the American Association of State Colleges and Universities.

Once again, those who don't know history are doomed to repeat it.

SOURCE: Art Levine, "America's Youthful Bigots," *U.S. News & World Report*, May 7, 1990.

MIDLIFE

Welcome to the Masquerade

Remember "adults"—those tall people you looked up to when you were eight? Then, you could hardly wait to be one. But when you turned eighteen, you didn't feel that much different than you did at sixteen—and when you turned twenty-one, you didn't feel that much different than at eighteen.

"You don't automatically grow up by a certain age, even if all the outer clues say you have," concludes Carin Rubenstein, Ph.D., after surveying 9,000 adults. As we move through our twenties, we begin to realize that being an adult is more complicated and takes longer than we ever dreamed. Being a grown-up, Rubenstein says, is a state of mind.

We'll never find a magical date or event that marks the passage from adolescence to adulthood. Most of us have to decide for ourselves when we have arrived. "Being married and owning a home do not guarantee that you have gained a sense of financial responsibility or learned to accept yourself," says Rubenstein. Perhaps that's why so many women and men she interviewed felt they were only masquerading as grown-ups.

SOURCE: Carin Rubenstein, "The New Adulthood," *Glamour*, April 1991.

The Procrastinator Gets the Worm

Not everyone enters adulthood at the same time. Some of us are early birds, others are procrastinators. However, when it comes to the age at which we attain maturity, it's the procrastinators who get the economic worm. The earlier we leave home, the less likely we are to complete a college education and the smaller our share of the economic pie.

People seem to believe they enter adulthood in four separate age brackets:

Early birds. 25 percent of us board the fast track to adulthood by the time we are eighteen, leaving home early and gaining our financial independence early, usually as a result of a parental divorce that forced us to begin earning our living earlier than most.

On-timers. 25 percent of us consider ourselves adults between our nineteenth and twenty-first birthdays, when we leave school and begin to support ourselves.

Procrastinators. About 35 percent of us have the luxury of taking our time growing up and only begin feeling a true sense of adulthood in our mid-twenties; procrastinators are more likely to graduate from college and hold white-collar jobs.

Late bloomers. About 15 percent of us don't feel like adults until our late twenties or early thirties; we live with our parents longer, hold the largest number of professional jobs, and have the highest incomes.

Although considered a serious character flaw, procrastination can have its financial rewards. "People who leave home later and marry later have the best outcome," explains demographer Martha Riche, Ph.D.

SOURCE: Ibid.; "The New Middle Age," *Newsweek*, December 7, 1992.

The New Generation Gap

Long after the era of the hippies, evidence of a generation gap is stronger than ever. Only it's not between adolescents and adults, but between young adults and senior citizens. And this time, instead of older people failing to understand the young, it's the young who don't understand the old.

Researchers at Long Island University wondered how differences in age affect our ability to understand each other. Women twenty-five to eighty watched videotapes (without any soundtrack) of women in the same age span describing events that had affected them strongly. Then participants were asked to guess what emotions the women on the tape had been feeling and how intensely they had been feeling them.

The greater the age gap, the fewer the number of correct guesses; the closer participants' ages were to those of the women on the videotape, the more accurate they were at reading what the other was feeling. Younger women had the most difficulty in reading the emotions of older women. Apparently the elderly understand the young better than the young understand their elders.

SOURCE: Malazesta, *Psychology and Aging*.

Shell-Shocked Urbanites

We often hear that our cities are becoming urban battlefields. Now a Henry Ford Hospital research project has produced evidence that "shell shock" is becoming endemic among young urban adults. The scientific name for shell shock, also known as "battle fatigue," is post-traumatic stress disorder (PTSD). Until the Ford survey, most victims were known to be combat vets, disaster and abuse survivors, and those who lost family members. Flashbacks and dreams of traumatic experiences, emotional numbness, paranoia, and difficulty concentrating haunt those who suffer from PTSD.

Almost 40 percent of the city dwellers surveyed had experienced these symptoms, while one in 10 actually developed PTSD. This makes PTSD one of the most common psychiatric disorders among young adults—only phobias, depression, and addiction outrank it. Triggers for PTSD include a spectrum of urban ills: sudden injury, serious accident, physical assault, rape, and seeing someone mugged or killed.

SOURCE: Bruce Bower "Trauma Disorder Strikes Many Young Adults," *Science News*, March 30, 1990.

The Golden Age of Sex

The Golden Age for sex seems to be our twenties and thirties, if a National Opinion Research Center survey can be believed. At that age couples seemed to reach a peak of sexual activity and inventiveness that far exceeded anything they experienced in their teens, or in subsequent decades, as revealed by these responses:

80 percent made love at least once a week.
70 percent enjoyed undressing each other.
55 percent engaged in sex outdoors.
46 percent went nude swimming together.

SOURCE: The National Opinion Research Center, *Newsweek*, August 24, 1992.

One Rotten Apple

How good is adult life? No better than its worst part, according to University of Michigan research. Most of us know our problems and negative feelings can carry over from one area of life to another. But a University of Michigan project involving men and women of all ages—from top-ranking executives to manual laborers and custodians—found that when we are unhappy in one area of life it makes us equally unhappy in all other areas. If you are only half-satisfied with your job or marriage, you'll only be half-satisfied with other aspects of your life.

SOURCE: "Life's Sore Spots," *Human Behavior*, January 1979.

What Was That?

Many companies dump older employees, convinced younger workers can bring greater concentration to their jobs. But a National Institute of Aging study found our minds don't wander more as they age—they become more focused. It's younger employees (twenty-one to forty) who can't keep their minds on the job at hand. We tend think more about the tasks we're doing and less about other matters as the decades pass. The younger participants were, the harder they found it to concentrate.

SOURCE: Paul Chance, "The Wandering Mind of Youth," *Psychology Today*, December 1988.

When You Don't Wish You Were Fifteen Again

It's an embarrassing condition that only afflicts adults. It can strike anyone from the age of twenty to ninety-nine at any time, and without any prior warning.

Therapists call it "regression," but to most of us it's feeling fifteen and foolish again. Social snubs, embarrassing mistakes, and being caught in a "little white lie" can all flood us with the kind of paralyzing shame and humiliation we experienced when we were made fools of as adolescents. Most adults thought they'd left these feelings behind with acne and puberty, and are horrified to find themselves hurled back to the worst moments of their teen years, says psychologist Judith Stone.

Our attacks of adolescent anguish will never completely disappear. But the second time around, they needn't be as devastating, Stone says. We know things as adults we didn't know as teens and can use this knowledge to place our feelings of being fifteen and foolish in perspective. We've had enough experience to realize we're going to win some and lose some in life—and will survive even the most painful humiliation.

SOURCE: Judith Stone, "Feeling Fifteen Again," *Glamour*, September 1990.

Prime Time or Middle Age?

According to psychologist Carin Rubenstein, tens of millions of adults were shocked to wake up one morning and discover a headlined wire service report in their newspapers announcing: "40 is middle aged." Many women and men in their forties must have felt their hearts stop.

Though the medical doctors quoted in the report defined forty as the beginning of middle age, other physicians and psychotherapists were quick to disagree. Though forty may have once represented middle age, today "we are seeing that fifty means all kinds of very vibrant, alive, sexy, dynamic people," says June Reinisch, director of the Kinsey Institute of Research in Sex, Gender, and Reproduction. Reinisch believes better health and increased life span are causing middle age to start later and last longer than for previous generations.

What we're really getting, Reinisch claims, is a second chance at youth, an unprecedented opportunity to live our lives over the way we wish we had. Unlike our parents' and grandparents' generation, we have 30 or more active years ahead of us after age forty and fifty. Women and men passing from their thirties are changing jobs, going back to school, renewing old relationships, seeking out new ones, and enjoying the leisure activities they've only dreamed of before (travel, sports, the arts). Instead of letting age define them, people today are redefining age, Reinisch says.

If true, we may soon think of life in our forties and beyond as prime time, not middle age.

SOURCE: Carin Rubenstein, "The New Adulthood," *Glamour*, April 1991.

Middle-Aged Mellow

When is losing your mind good for you? When it helps you say farewell to worry. Between the ages of forty and sixty, we lose many of the brain cells that register anxiety, according to research cited in a *Newsweek* special report. No wonder men and women are reported to mellow when they reach middle age. Because our brain cells are dying, says Ronald Kessler of the Institute for Social Research, in terms of mental health, midlife is also prime time.

SOURCE: "The New Middle Age," *Newsweek*, December 7, 1992.

Keeping Up Appearances

The baby boomers have enjoyed the most prolonged period of youth and vigor known to any generation in history. But now as age finally catches up with them, many have turned to rigorous nutritional regimes, Eastern meditation, even hair colorings and plastic surgery, to try to postpone the dreaded specter of old age. University of California at Los Angeles gerontologist Fernando Torres-Gil predicts boomers won't truly confront old age until they are in their seventies.

Mel Bircoll, M.D., the father of modern cosmetic surgery, backs up Torres-Gil's assertions. Boomers are showing up in his office more frequently, Bircoll says, as the average age of his clients has dropped from fifty-five to forty-five. An American Society of Plastic and Reconstructive Surgeons survey found 27 percent of all face-lifts were in the boomers' thirty-five to fifty age bracket; while boomers received 64 percent of all tummy-tucks. In their quest for youth, more than 1 million boomers now shell out more than $5 million for cosmetic surgery each year.

For boomers, keeping up with the Joneses seems to mean keeping up appearances.

SOURCE: Ibid.

MATURITY

How Old Is Old?

When does old age begin? Don't ask scientists—they can't seem to agree. One school of thought suggests old age is the point when the expected remaining years of life is 10. Another believes old age should be divided into the young-old and the old-old because the needs and interests of the two groups diverge widely. A third defines old age as seventy-five and above. A fourth sets it at eighty to eighty-five. Others argue the term itself is meaningless. If this controversy continues, many now living will die of old age before scientists agree on what it is.

SOURCE: Birren and Schaie, *Psychology of Aging.*

The Time of Our Lives

The summers seem longer when we are children. The period between one New Year's Day and another feels as if it stretches on forever. But as adults, each new year comes so quickly it catches us by surprise, and we wonder where the months have gone. By the time we become senior citizens, half a year seems to go by in a blur—the years whip past at a breathless rate. The seeming acceleration of time is a natural phenomenon. Experiments show time seems to pass more slowly when we are unoccupied. As children, with so little that's urgent filling our attention, the days appear to pass slowly. But as our preoccupations increase throughout adulthood, even the minutes seem crowded, creating the illusion that time passes faster and faster with age.

SOURCE: John Boslough, "The Enigma of Time," *National Geographic*, March 1990.

They'd Rather Be Right

We all know women and men who remain mentally alert and in full possession of their faculties throughout their lives. Then there are others who experience a continuing mental erosion once they pass their prime. Scientists long sought a physical explanation for these differences: health, heredity, exercise. However, a three-decade study by psychologist Warner Schaie suggests the cause may be more psychological than physiological.

Remaining alive, bright, and alert as we age, Schaie found, resulted from a flexible, open-minded attitude toward life. Rigid, closed-minded, and dogmatic men and women experienced significant deterioration of intelligence, alertness, memory, and personality as they grew older. But when the closed-minded could be open-minded enough to embrace flexibility, Schaie discovered, they regained a large measure of their mental powers, no matter how advanced their age. However, those willing to change represent only a minute fraction of the rigid and dogmatic, Schaie concedes. As for the rest, apparently they'd rather be right than bright.

SOURCE: Jeff Meer, "Mental Alertness and the Good Old Days," *Psychology Today*, March 1985.

Exercising the Memory

Concerned about your memory fading as you grow older? Don't be. There's a simple solution: strengthen your memory by strengthening your body. A Scripps College research project involving women and men aged fifty-five to eighty-nine found those who exercised for just 12 minutes a day developed better memories, quicker reactions, and more accurate reasoning.

Psychologists Louise Carkson-Smith and Alan A. Hartley, who supervised the study, concluded that regular exercise may forestall some of the bad effects of age on the central nervous system.

SOURCE: Robert J. Trotter, "Exercise: Getting Your Head in Shape," *Psychology Today*, January 1988.

No Lost Horizons

Recent research suggests adults may not experience any loss of mental ability as they age, as previous studies had suggested. It wasn't older people's minds that were faulty—it was the tests they were given. Previous tests compared senior citizens with students, a group unusually adept in the tricks that aid memorization. When later studies compared adults in their twenties and thirties to students, they too appeared to be experiencing a decline in memory. What had actually declined, researchers realized, wasn't adults' memory, but their degree of proficiency with the tricks of the memory trade. This news should cheer seniors who fear a decline in their mental faculties.

SOURCE: Jeff Meer, "The Reason of Age," *Psychology Today*, June 1986.

Peaceful (Day) Dreams

We not only daydream less as we grow older, we daydream differently. As we age, psychological and physical changes make us less aggressive and less willing to extend ourselves physically in risky situations—and our daydreams reflect these changes. Hostile and heroic themes—fantasies of saving a drowning child, blowing away terrorists, physically hurting an enemy, telling off the boss—all show a sharp decline. College-age women and men told psychologist Leonard Giambra, Ph.D., they usually had such fantasies, while those over sixty-five reported this was not true or usually not true of them. These findings may give pause to whose who have argued that we would benefit from seeking a younger crop of politicians.

SOURCE: Leonard Giambra, "Daydreaming Across the Lifespan," *Journal of Aging and Human Development*, Vol. 5.

A Matter of Motivation

Images of the young as highly motivated go-getters and of seniors as burned-out husks may be due for revision. While motivation does dip in our late fifties and early sixties, studies show it rebounds sharply thereafter, says psychologist David Kausler. Motivation was found to decrease between the ages of fifty-five and sixty-nine, and then increase again during our seventies. It dropped once more in the early eighties, and returned for a last hurrah between eighty-five and ninety. Companies in search of highly motivated personnel might find a vast resource among this extremely underused labor pool.

SOURCE: Kausler, "Motivation."

The Furnace Is Still Fine, Thank You!

Sex is better than ever for a surprisingly large number of seniors. Data from 6,000 respondents age sixty and over revealed that 37 percent still have intercourse at least once a week. Almost three-fourths admitted they frequently indulged in caressing without intercourse; half engaged in self-gratification and masturbation; and more than half confessed they still had vivid sexual daydreams. One out of 6 even reported sex had become more enjoyable and satisfying. Encouragingly, only a third reported no interest in sex whatsoever. Apparently, sex remains alive and well into our sixties and beyond.

SOURCE: Paul McCarthy, "Ageless Sex," *Psychology Today*, March 1989; Kenneth L. Woodward and Karen Springer, "Better Than a Gold Watch," *Newsweek*, August 24, 1992.

The Best Revenge

How does race affect old age? Statistics paint a grim picture for many members of minority groups in youth. Then, in the final two decades of life, minority group members pull ahead in longevity, self-esteem, and health.

Research shows significant differences in the life span and older age experiences of ethnic minorities—blacks, Native Americans, Hispanics, Asians—in the U.S. and Europe. Negative environmental, social, and economic conditions early in life result in shortened life expectancy, premature aging, earlier retirement, increased illness, and higher rates of suicide, accidents, and death. Minorities are also at higher risk for many mental illnesses, particularly paranoia, suicide, and depression.

However, at age eighty and beyond, an ironic reversal takes place. Though many minority members have died along the way, survivors begin to live longer and to be healthier than members of majority cultures. Ironically, at this age their self-esteem outstrips that of majority members, and so does their mental health.

SOURCE: Jackson, "Cultural, Racial, and Ethnic Minority Influences."

Who's a Contrasexual?

Are you a contrasexual? If you aren't, you will be, according to psychologist David Gutman of Northwestern University.

Men become more nurturing and family oriented, while women become more independent and aggressive as they pass middle age, claims Gutman. Psychiatrist Carl Jung called this reversal of attitude and behavior the "contrasexual transition." According to cross cultural surveys by Gutman, contrasexuality is a universal phenomenon. Thousands of seniors in dozens of cultures and countries are becoming contrasexuals every day.

SOURCE: Gutman, *Reclaimed Powers.*

It's True What They Say About Older People

There's reassuring news—for some at least. Most of us really do become wiser as the years pass, according to research involving thousands of older adults conducted at Berlin's Max Planck Institute for Human Development and Education. The researchers defined wisdom as possession of:

- A rich factual knowledge about life.
- The ability to perceive life in context.
- Composure in coping with the uncertainties of life.

The acquisition of wisdom is not guaranteed by age, researchers discovered. Many seniors are far from wise. But overall, they found the older individuals were, the wiser they had become.

SOURCE: Simonton, "Creativity and Wisdom in Aging."

More Amazing Facts About the Mind

A Short Primer on Sleep

The High Price of Sleep

We sleep one-third of our lives away. More than 25 of our allotted 80 years are lost in slumber. That's more than 10,000 days or 240,000 hours. If you could keep awake and work those quarter of a million hours, even at minimum wage, you'd have an additional $1 million to count instead of sheep.

SOURCE: Matt Clark, et al., "The Mystery of Sleep," *Newsweek*, July 13, 1981.

Mother Nature's Bodyguard

If we were reptiles we would have no need to sleep. Snakes, lizards, and toads never sleep. But they are helplessly dependent on the sun for much of the body heat that keeps them alive and active. At night, and on dark cloudy days, reptiles become dormant. Helpless and unable to move quickly, they are easy prey for nocturnal predators.

Nature's response is warm-blooded animals that maintain their own source of body heat. But the internal fires that generate that heat need to be constantly stoked with food, and conserved when possible. Researcher Stephen LaBerge, Ph.D., believes our bodies sleep to conserve the energy that would otherwise be spent keeping us warm at night, though, unlike reptiles, we can rouse instantly and flee nocturnal predators if threatened.

"Sleep," according to LaBerge, is "mother nature's way of keeping you off the streets after dark, and out of trouble."

SOURCE: LaBerge, *Lucid Dreaming.*

Try Counting These Instead of Sheep

Many of us take sleep for granted. We slip under the covers, lay there a while, and drift off. But sleep deprivation is a serious problem for many men and women. Sleep researchers have identified 60 different sleep disorders that affect hundreds of millions around the world. Insomnia alone plagues an estimated 1 out of every 8 women and men.

Among the more common sleep disorders are: sleeping only during the day; insomnia; sleeping too much; sleeping too little; disrupted sleep-wake schedule; poor-quality sleep; falling asleep late and waking up late; going to sleep early and waking up early; sleepwalking; sleeptalking, dream-anxiety attacks; teeth grinding; and night terror.

Sleep disorders can be hereditary. But some occupations demand such irregular sleeping schedules that even those who aren't prone to sleep disorders develop them: airline pilots, soldiers, long-distance truck drivers, newspaper reporters and editors, night and swing shift workers, firefighters, doctors, nurses, and police.

Sleep disorders are a serious health problem that is not being recognized says Harvey Moldofsky, M.D., chief of psychiatry at the Toronto Western Hospital's Sleep Disorders Clinic. Disrupted sleep can result in confusion, disorientation, memory loss, mood swings, violent anger, depression, stress, heart problems, and even hallucinations and psychosis.

SOURCE: Rae Corelli, "The Mysteries of Sleep and Dreams," *Macleans*, April 23, 1990.

Sleepyheads

Are you tired? Do you find it hard to wake up in the morning and stay alert during the day? If so, you're in the same boat as more than half the world's population. Most adults need 8.3 hours of sleep at a minimum, claims William Dement, M.D., of the Stanford University Medical School. But typically, keyed up by the day's stresses, we catch the 11 P.M. news, a bit of a late-night talk show, and then fall asleep near midnight, only to wake at 5 or 6 A.M. to start all over again. As a result, we don't get enough sleep at night. "Most adults are substantially sleepy all the time." says William Dement.

SOURCE: Matt Clark, et al., "The Mystery of Sleep," *Newsweek*, July 13, 1981.

Blue Monday

Many of us get the Monday morning blues, though some of us are more susceptible to it than others. They strike like clockwork in the first waking moments of the first day of the business week. Scientists long thought the condition was psychological, caused by our natural reluctance to return to the daily grind.

But now researchers at Germany's Max Planck Institute have uncovered a surprising new explanation for our Monday morning blues. Though the world revolves on a 24-hour cycle, our bodies operate on a natural 25-hour day. Many of us try to compensate for the hour of sleep we lose during the work week by going to bed an hour or two earlier on Friday and Saturday nights.

By the time Monday morning rolls around, our bodies have reverted to their normal 25-hour cycle, and need that extra hour of sleep we can't give them. We wake up feeling groggy, listless, out of sorts—in short, we've got the Monday blues.

SOURCE: Ibid.

Sleepwalking

If you've never sleepwalked, it's not for lack of trying. Our bodies try to sleepwalk every night, but are restrained by a special center in the brain. When you walk, talk, move, and eat in a dream, your brain sends the same signals to your body that it does when you do them in waking life, Stephen LaBerge, Ph.D., a Stanford sleep researcher, claims.

But for a handful of men and women, the brain center that keeps us immobilized during our dreams goes haywire, at least some of the time. While still asleep, these people open their eyes, get out of bed, walk around, even eat and perform chores. But they can't remember anything of these nocturnal excursions when they wake up.

Sleepwalking is more common during childhood and adolescence—perhaps because the brain mechanism that keeps the body immobile hasn't finished forming yet. Sleepwalking is supposed to be rare in adults. But it's possible scientists may be mistaken in performing their research at night. According to many employers, there's anecdotal evidence that a large number of employees are to be found sleepwalking during the day.

SOURCE: LaBerge, *Lucid Dreaming*.

Sleep-Talking

While the idea of talking out loud in our sleep may seem like a bad plot device in a comedy, everyone does it. Scientists call this phenomenon "sleep-talking."

Everyone's heard of sleepwalking. Yet sleep-talking is far more common: More than 70 percent of us sleep-talk. Few of us realize just how common sleep-talking is because all the witnesses are asleep.

SOURCE: McCutcheon, *Compass in Your Nose.*

A Dreamy Discovery

The science of modern sleep research stems from an accident so unlikely its youthful discoverer almost threw out the results. In 1953 Eugene Aserinsky, a doctoral candidate working on his Ph.D. thesis at the University of Chicago, decided to tape electrodes near sleepers' eyes and use an electroencephalograph (EEG) to record the movement. The only EEG available was a broken-down machine that had long ago been abandoned in a university basement.

For weeks, Aserinsky struggled to put the malfunctioning EEG in working condition. "It would break down with one ailment and I would fix that, and it would break down with something else," he says. Just when Aserinsky thought the balky EEG was completely repaired, he noticed that sometimes it stopped making the slow, smooth lines associated with eye movements during sleep and started producing the sharp peaks and valleys created when we look around consciously while awake.

Until then, scientists thought the sleeping brain was completely inactive—except for the subconscious processes involved in maintaining vital physiological systems like breathing, heartbeat, and blood pressure. Aserinsky decided there must be still something wrong with his EEG and tried calling the machine's manufacturer and the leading scientific authority on the use of the EEG. Neither could help and they both advised abandoning the project.

Aserinsky began to panic. "If I had a suicidal nature, this would have been the time. I was married, I had a child, I'd been in universities for 12 years with no degree to show for it. I'd already spent a couple of years horsing around on this. I was absolutely finished."

Aserinsky was left with two possibilities: Either his advisors were right, and in spite of all the tests and repairs he'd made, there was still something wrong with his EEG—or he had made an important scientific discovery and the brain produced previously unsuspected bursts of activity during sleep. Was there any way to determine which? Finally Aserinsky saw the solution: He could record the movements of one eye on his machine and the other eye on a machine known to be in perfect working condition. Since both eyes moved in tandem, if the second machine showed the same jagged lines at the same time, he'd have proof that his records had been accurate and sleepers' eyes were actually moving.

Borrowing a second machine briefly from a colleague, Aserinsky soon proved we do experience episodes of rapid eye movement (REM sleep) throughout the night. The results earned him his Ph.D. and world fame. The young doctoral candidate had unwittingly laid the foundations for the modern science of sleep and dream research.

SOURCE: Edward Dolnick, "What Dreams Are (Really) Made Of," *Atlantic Monthly*, July 1990.

BITS AND PIECES

Where Does the Time Go?

More than half of our life is a waste of time. That's the message of a study by Michael Fortino of Priority Management, a time management company. During our lifetime, we spend:

· Five years standing in line.
· Two years trying to return telephone calls.
· Eight months opening direct mail.
· Six years eating.
· One year looking for misplaced objects.
· Four years doing household chores.
· Twenty-five years sleeping.

Out of an 80-year span, 43 are taken up by trivial, boring tasks that occupy most of our free time. Another 20 years are consumed by work. Out of the 30,000 or so days of our lives, how many are devoted to the pursuit of our own interests and satisfaction? A mere 6,000, or 17 years. Fortino's studies give new credibility to the philosophy of making every minute count.

SOURCE: John Boslough, "The Enigma of Time," *National Geographic*, March, 1990.

The 28-Hour Day

Many of us have heard people say, If only there were more hours in the day. Chances are you've said it yourself. What would you do if you could fit more hours into your day? One university survey asked several hundred men and women what they would do if they had four more hours in the day. Their answers were:

- 33 percent: Read.
- 31 percent: Fix things around the house.
- 27 percent: Pursue hobbies.
- 26 percent: Socialize.
- 21 percent: Exercise.
- 14 percent: Sleep.
- 12 percent: Study.
- 12 percent: Organize.
- 8 percent: Cook.
- 4 percent: Daydream.
- 3 percent: Work.
- 3 percent: Eat.
- 1 percent: Hold a second job.

Ironically romance and sex did not even make the list.

SOURCE: "Crosstalk," *Psychology Today*, March 1989.

What Scares Us?

What are the things that scare us most? Murder? War? The threat of global extinction from toxic pollution? Higher taxes? Lower taxes?

A survey conducted by the Roper Organization, a public opinion firm asked interviewees what frightened them most in our modern world. The researchers pronounced themselves "astonished" at the results:

- 41 percent: Snakes.
- 26 percent: Public speaking.
- 19 percent: High, open spaces.
- 16 percent: Mice.
- 16 percent: Flying in a plane.
- 11 percent: Spiders and insects.

Respondents apparently found themselves most frightened of things that affected their daily lives, instead of long-range future possibilities like war and global threats.

SOURCE: "Crosstalk," *Psychology Today*, November 1988.

What Makes You Happy?

Polls have revealed a great deal about our dissatisfactions. But what makes us feel good? A group of scientists decided to find out.

The results suggest a positive shift in personal values during the second half of the twentieth century. Asked to list the things that made them happiest, the men and women surveyed gave the following responses:

- 32 percent: Family and friends.
- 20 percent: Hobbies and entertainment.
- 13 percent: Accomplishments.

- 10 percent: Nature.
- 4 percent: Health.
- 3 percent: Food.
- 3 percent: Money.
- 3 percent: Surprises.
- 1 percent: Sex.

Instead of being at the top of the list, money and sex ranked at the bottom while most respondents picked family and friends as their greatest source of happiness.

SOURCE: "Happiness Is . . . ," *Psychology Today*, November 1988.

Warning Signs of Family Homicide

Family members slay each other with increasing frequency these days. But when those involved are aware of the warning signs, they can often head off a murderous outburst by a relative or loved one, says magazine editor Robert Trotter.

What factors are typically present when family members kill family members? According to those who have studied family homicide, it is most frequently associated with:

- Drug use by perpetrator.
- Alcohol use by perpetrator.
- Perpetrator under strong cultural pressures to save face or prove himself or herself powerful or in control.
- Previous threats of suicide by perpetrator.
- Perpetrator suffered recent deep depression.
- Perpetrator suffered recent failed love relationship.
- Perpetrator recently separated from family unit.
- Vengeful threats previously made by perpetrator.

SOURCE: Robert Trotter, "Psychology in Action," *Psychology Today*, November 1987.

Nature's Way of Saying "High"

There are hundreds, perhaps even thousands, of drugs, natural and synthetic, that people take to alter their minds and bodies. And new ones are being designed every day. But there are really only six basic classes of drugs (whether occurring in nature or created in the lab):

- **Euphorics.** Produce a feeling of well-being (marijuana, opium, heroin).
- **Psychoactives.** Generate unearthly experiences and visions (LSD, Methylenedioxymethamphetamine, peyote).
- **Inebriants.** Cause intoxication (alcohol, nitrous oxide).
- **Sedatives.** Dull us to calmness and sleep (barbiturates, methaqualone).
- **Stimulants.** Produce alertness and arousal (amphetamines, caffeine).
- **Ataraxics.** Create tranquilization without drowsiness (Thorazine, Mellaril, Prolixin).

Why do we live in an environment saturated with drugs? Pychopharmacologist Andrew Weil, M.D., believes he has the answer. The cross-cultural and cross-species evidence, Weil claims, suggests all mammalian species have a natural urge to get high.

SOURCE: De Ropp, *Drugs and the Mind.*

Reading Lesson

Have trouble reading people? At a loss for a clue as to what others are feeling? Reading people is easy if you know how, says psychologist Patricia Maybruck, Ph.D. Every strong emotion gives itself away in the form of unmistakable physical clues.

If you want to know what people are feeling, you don't have to be another Sigmund Freud—all you have to do is keep an eye out for the following physical signs. Each is an unmistakable indicator of the emotions that produce it.

Emotion	Physical Signs
Anger (fury, indignation, wrath, resentment, frustration, annoyance)	Increased heart rate and blood pressure; rapid deep breathing; indigestion; flushed face; erect hair; muscle strength; increased brain activity (speeded-up thoughts).
Fear (terror, fright, panic, alarm, dread, anxiety, nervousness)	Increased heart rate; lower blood pressure; slower brain activity; loss of bladder and bowel control; pale face; cool or clammy sweat; rapid, shallow breathing.
Pain (agony, suffering, hurt feelings, sorrow, grief, distress)	Muscle tension; abdominal, pelvis, and groin spasms; blurred vision; tears; dizziness; ragged breathing; irregular heart rate, blood pressure, high temperature, and other symptoms of shock; incoherent speech.
Pleasure and love (happiness, contentment, joy, desire, passion)	Relaxed muscles; steady, even breathing; absence of tension; smiles; giggles; sexual arousal; overall well-being.

SOURCE: Maybruck, *Pregnancy and Dreams.*

Familiar Faces

There's good news for rejected lovers. Familiarity, it turns out, doesn't breed contempt. It makes the heart grow fonder.

The more often we see, taste, smell, and hear something or someone, the more we like it, according to researchers. These findings may explain why some people have married, even though they found their prospective spouse unappealing at first. It also may explain why we find those of our own country and race more attractive than members of other groups. It may also explain the effectiveness of many otherwise obnoxious advertising campaigns.

SOURCE: John F. Kihlstrom, "The Cognitive Unconscious," *Science*, September 18, 1987.

No Laughing Matter

The funniest people in the world are also the saddest, according to at least one researcher. The great comedians—whose comic pratfalls and droll wit set the world laughing—become withdrawn and despondent the moment they step out of the limelight. Psychiatrist Samuel Janus persuaded 55 successful comics to participate in personality profiles. Janus's conclusions? The vast majority of comics and clowns are sad people who suffer from major depression. If we listen closely to their routines, Janus claims, "many of our top comedians are really crying out loud."

SOURCE: Maisel, *Staying Sane*.

The Secret of Productivity

What's the secret of productivity? Start early. Opt for quantity over quality. That's the answer suggested by research cited by psychologists James Birren and Warner Schaie.

Studies of productive women and men in business, science, politics, and the arts revealed they shared three key characteristics. They all:

· Began their careers at early ages.
· Continued working at late ages.
· Produced at extraordinary rates throughout their careers.

High, continuous productivity apparently boosts self-esteem, which boosts endorphins, which in turn generate high energy and a sense of well-being that rekindles our urge to produce—leading to further productivity and the repetition of the cycle.

SOURCE: Birren and Schaie, *Psychology of Aging*.

Why You Can't Do Two Things at Once

It's true. You can't do two things at once—at least not well. The brain simply isn't built that way.

Experiments by psychologist Harold Pashler, Ph.D., at the University of California at San Diego showed we are unable mentally to track two different tasks, even if both are very simple. Women and men were asked to label an object with their right hand while pushing a button with their left every time they heard a certain musical note. Response time to the tone was delayed if it came in the midst of labeling; labeling was always slowed while participants pushed the button. One task was always delayed while the conscious mind dealt with the other.

Scientists call this "dual-task interference." And Pashler claims it has an important message for everyone. "When expected to perform two tasks," he says, "don't bother starting on the second before you have performed the first."

SOURCE: Harold Pashler, "Conversation Stopper," *Psychology Today*, September/October 1992.

The Long and the Short of It

We like tall people more than we like short people. It's not something most of us are willing to believe about ourselves, but hundreds of studies back it up. American society operates on the premise that to be tall is to be good and to be short is to be inadequate, according to psychologist Gordon Patzer, Ph.D. Phrases like "a giant among men (or women)" and "belittling someone" give unwitting testimony to this prejudice.

For some reason, we tend to be biased in favor of taller people. As John Kenneth Galbraith, the 6-foot, 8-inch economist remarked, one of our most blatant and forgiven prejudices is the bias in favor of height. In a series of experiments cited by Patzer, groups of college students were introduced to a person who was made to look taller or shorter through the use of lighting, platform shoes, and stance. The higher the students estimated the person's height, the higher they rated that person's physical attractiveness.

Short people have more to worry about than a Randy Newman song, store shelves that are out of range, and slacks that are too long. They are one minority group still unwittingly derided by the media. Shorter men are often characterized as small, pallid, and bland, while shorter women are described as short, wiry, and frenetic.

To overcome society's biases and win its approval despite her or his height—a short person apparently has to ride pretty tall in the saddle.

SOURCE: Patzer, *Physical Attractiveness Phenomenon.*

It's a Real Boon to the Antacid Companies, Though

If you find yourself racing through your meal at a restaurant, it may be due to the music. Savvy restaurateurs are picking up the tempo—of the music, that is. Slow, soothing music is out, ragtime is in.

It's all the result of an experiment by psychologist Elizabeth Gardner, who experimented with music in company cafeterias. When there was no music playing, diners consumed an average 3.23 bites per minute; with slow instrumental music the rate increased to 3.83 bites per minute; but when fast instrumental music was heard, it soared all the way to 4.4 bites per minute.

When ragtime played patrons were eating more than 25 percent faster. For restaurateurs concerned about the bottom line, increasing the tempo of the music they play seems to promise a bonanza: The faster patrons eat, the more customers per hour a restaurant can accommodate.

There was a word of caution in a follow-up study Gardner conducted at a local restaurant. Although faster music did cause people to eat faster, they still spent the same amount of time at the table. They merely lingered longer afterwards, socializing over coffee and dessert.

SOURCE: Paul Chance, "Danger: Different Drummer," *Psychology Today*, November 1988.

A Tip About Touching

Looking for a raise? Need a loan? Want your spouse to okay an extravagant personal indulgence? Getting what you want may be easier than you think. Just put "the touch" on others. Research into the effect of touch on tipping conducted by psychologists April Crusco and Christopher Wetzel may have given this shopworn cliché new meaning.

In one restaurant study, customers were chosen at random, and the waitresses serving them were asked to touch them lightly on the palm or shoulder. Women and men who were touched—even if the touch was so light they were unaware of it—left bigger tips than the patrons who were not touched.

SOURCE: Richard Camer, "Gratuitous Touching," *Psychology Today*, April 1985.

The Phony Smile

Many of us have heard someone described as having a phony smile. Now science has proven that some smiles really are phony—they don't even come from the same part of the brain that creates happy smiles. Studies of patients who were paralyzed on one side found that when they were asked to smile, they were unable to produce even a poor smile on the paralyzed side, according to neuropsychiatrist Norman Geschwind. But when these patients were happy or something struck them as funny, a spontaneous smile spread across their faces. This led Geschwind to conclude that we have "a region in the depths of the brain which contains the innate program for smiling." Although the stroke patients had no conscious control over their faces, Geschwind explains, the region in the brain that generates genuine smiles was still intact and in communication with the facial muscles.

SOURCE: Hooper and Teresi, *3-Pound Universe*.

Seeing Things

Pigeons hallucinate red dots. Monkeys hallucinate food. But what do people hallucinate? Psychologist Ronald Siegel of UCLA has spent years mapping our hallucinatory never-never land in an attempt to find out.

Siegel's painstaking surveys reveal a colorful fantasia of optical illusions generated when the brain plays tricks on the eye:

- Black, white, and violet hues were seen frequently during meditation, relaxation, and trance.
- Red, orange, and yellow predominated under the influence of many psychedelics.
- Cool blues were reported by those exposed to THC (tetrahydrocannabinol), the active ingredient in marijuana.
- Increasingly intricate geometric shapes were produced by LSD (lysergic acid diethylamide) and mescaline.
- Random black and white forms reported as boring to watch resulted from depressants, amphetamines, and placebos.

SOURCE: Talbot, *Holographic Universe*.

A Close Look at Intelligence

Men and women who wear glasses are often perceived as being smarter. Images of brainy bespectacled students lugging around armloads of books have been with us ever since glasses were invented. The youthful-looking even don eyewear they don't need, just to appear more mature.

Scientists have long ridiculed the premise behind this myth. Why should there be more smart people among those born with poor eyesight, they argued, than there are among those born with long legs? But two independent research projects have unearthed evidence of just such a link.

Israeli researchers Mordechai Rosner and Michael Belkin surveyed 150,000 Israeli military recruits. Those who wore glasses were almost always the brightest and best educated. A survey of gifted junior high school students led by psychologist Sanford Cohn also found spectacles perched on the noses of the brainiest. Neither group of researchers had an explanation for this link.

The answer may lie in brain structure. Until further studies are done, all scientists are willing to say is there's more to the myth of the nearsighted genius than meets the eye.

SOURCE: Laurence Miller, "The Real Revenge of the Nerds," *Psychology Today*, June 1989.

A New Cure for the Disorganized

We usually call people whose minds constantly flit from subject to subject "disorganized." But their minds may actually be giving them a jump start on organization.

Our brains are wired to resist sticking to a single topic for very long, claims researcher Eric Klinger, Ph.D. Despite our best efforts to concentrate on the task at hand, about half the time our thoughts jump around randomly.

Instead of making us less organized, this seeming mental disorganization helps us stay organized. Our minds keep coming back to the subjects that concern us most, Klinger says. This constant recycling of our thoughts helps keep us from forgetting the most important of our commitments, agendas, and priorities.

SOURCE: Klinger, *Daydreaming*.

Ask and Ye Shall Receive

Faced with an insoluble problem? Desperate for inspiration? An article in *Prevention* offers the following suggestions for tapping your creative unconscious:

1. Find a quiet, relaxing spot.
2. Close your eyes and imagine you are in the presence of the wisest person in the world—picture him or her as vividly as you can.
3. Ask this wise person a question concerning a problem you have.

Many people are surprised at the accuracy of the answers this technique produces, according to the article. Questions aren't always answered directly. Sometimes your question may be answered with another question. That's to help you see the problem in a different light, the author explains. Usually this will get you started thinking in a whole new direction.

SOURCE: Mark Golin, "Tapping the Wise Man Within," *Prevention*, May 1988.

Three Types of Personality

How complex are we? Considering how bewildering so many human actions are—and the seeming infinite levels and nuances of the mind—one would probably guess we're pretty complex animals.

But we're actually fairly simple to figure out, claims Minnesota psychologist Auke Tellegen. All the aspects of our personalities boil down to just three basic characteristics. In Tellegen's view, the elements that give our characters their distinctive shapes are the degrees to which we display:

- **Positive effectivity.** The amount of good feeling we experience.

- **Negative effectivity.** The amount of anxious, tense feelings we experience.

- **Constraint.** The amount of self-control we feel it necessary to exercise.

And there you have it, the optimistic and the pessimistic in the first two; the liberal and conservative in the third. From their conflicts and interactions have grown our personalities, philosophies, wars, and social institutions.

SOURCE: Klinger, *Daydreaming.*

For Further Reading

Books

Among the books consulted in the preparation of this work were:

Aftel, Mandy, and Robin Tolmach Lakoff. *When Talk Is Not Cheap or How to Find the Right Therapist When You Don't Know Where to Begin*. Warner, 1985.

American Psychiatric Association. *Psychiatric Manpower for the 80s*. American Psychiatric Association Press, 1980.

Asimov, Isaac. *The Brain*. Houghton Mifflin, 1963.

Batten, Mary. *Sexual Strategies: How Females Choose Their Mates*. Tarcher, 1992.

Beigel, Hugo. "The Meaning of Coital Positions." In *Sexual Behavior and Personality Characteristics*, edited by Manfred De Martino. Grove, 1966.

Benson, Herbert. *The Relaxation Response*. Morrow, 1975.

Birren, James, and Warner Schaie. *Handbook of the Psychology of Aging*. Academic Press, 1990.

Bloomfield, Harold. "The Healing Silence." In *Healers on Healing*, edited by Richard Carlson and Benjamin Shield. Tarcher, 1989.

Brown, Barbara. *Stress and the Art of Biofeedback*. Bantam, 1978.

Budge, H. S. *Dimensions of Physical Attractiveness*. 1981 unpublished doctoral dissertation, University of Utah, Salt Lake City.

Calder, Nigel. *The Mind of Man*. Viking, 1970.

Campbell, Don. *Introduction to the Musical Brain*. Magnamusic Baton, Inc., 1983.

Chamberlain, David. *Babies Remember Birth and Other Extraordinary Scientific Discoveries About the Mind and Personality of Your Newborn.* Tarcher, 1988.

Columbia University College of Physicians and Surgeons. *Complete Home Medical Guide.* Crown Publishers, 1985.

Compton's Encyclopedia and Fact Finder, Encyclopaedia Britannica Inc., 1991.

DeRopp, Robert. *Drugs and the Mind.* Grove, 1961.

DeVillers, Linda. "Loveskills."

————. Letter, January 29, 1993.

Duncan, Ronald, and Miranda Weston-Smith. *The Encyclopaedia of Ignorance.* Pocket, 1977.

Elkind, David. *The Hurried Child.* Addison-Wesley, 1990.

Fishman, Steve. *A Bomb in the Brain.*

Frank, Janrae. "Women at Arms." Unpublished manuscript, 1993.

Frey, William, and Saleed Salameh, eds. *Handbook of Humor and Psychotherapy.* Professional Resource Exchange, 1986.

Gerbrer, Albert. *The Book of Sex Lists.* Lyle Stuart, 1981.

Gilligan, Carol. *In a Different Voice: Psychological Theory and Women's Development.* Harvard University Press, Cambridge, Mass., 1982.

Globus, Gordon. "The Causal Theory of Perception: A Critique and Revision Through Reflection on Dreams." In *Consciousness and the Brain.* Plenum, 1976.

Goleman, Daniel. *Vital Lies, Simple Truths.* Simon and Schuster, 1986.

Gosselin, Christopher, and Glenn Wilson. *Sexual Variations.* Faber and Faber, 1980.

Grossvogel, David. *Dear Ann Landers.* Simon and Schuster, 1987.

Gutman, David. *Reclaimed Powers: Toward a New Psychology of Men and Women in Later Life.* University of Iowa Press, 1983.

Haley, Jay. "The Art of Being a Failure as a Therapist." In *The Power Tactics of Jesus Christ and Other Essays.* Grossman, 1969.

Hampden-Turner, Charles. *Maps of the Mind.* Macmillan, 1981.

Harman, Willis, and Howard Rheingold. *Higher Creativity.* Tarcher, 1984.

Heller, Joseph, and William A. Henkin. *Bodywise: Regaining Your Natural Flexibility and Vitality for Maximum Well-Being.* Tarcher, 1986.

Hoffman, Mark S., ed. *The World Almanac and Book of Facts 1993.* Pharos Books, 1992.

Hofstadter, Douglas R., and Daniel C. Dennett, eds. *The Mind's I: Fantasies and Reflections on Self and Soul.* Basic, 1981.

Hooper, Judith, and Dick Teresi. *The 3-Pound Universe.* Tarcher, 1991.

Jackson, James. "Cultural, Racial, and Ethnic Minority Influences on Aging." In *Handbook of the Psychology of Aging,* ed. James E.

Birren and K. Warner Schaie, Third edition. Academic Press, Inc., 1990.

Justice, Blair. *Who Gets Sick: How Beliefs, Moods, and Thought Affect Your Health.* Tarcher, 1988.

Kaplan, Helen Singer. Ph.D. paper read at a meeting of the Los Angeles Chapter of the Society for the Scientific Study of Sex, December 1990.

Karlen, Arno. *Threesomes: Studies in Sex, Power, and Intimacy.* Beech Tree Books, 1988.

Kausler, David. "Motivation, Human Aging, and Cognitive Performance." In *Handbook of the Psychology of Aging,* ed. James E. Birren and K. Warner Schaie, Third edition. Academic Press, Inc., 1990.

Klein, Allen. *The Healing Power of Humor.* Tarcher, 1989.

Klimo, John. *Channeling.* Tarcher, 1987.

Klinger, Eric. *Daydreaming.* Tarcher, 1990.

Kottler, Jeffrey. *Private Moments, Secret Selves: Enriching Our Time Alone.* Tarcher, 1990.

Krakow, Barry. *Conquering Bad Dreams and Nightmares.* Berkeley, 1990.

LaBerge, Stephen. *Lucid Dreaming.* Bantam, 1986.

Light, Donald. *Becoming a Psychiatrist.* Norton, 1980.

Louis, David. *1001 Fascinating Facts.* Greenhouse House, 1983.

Lowenfield, Margaret. *Children and Play.*

McCutcheon, Marc. *The Compass in Your Nose: And Other Astonishing Facts About Humans.* Tarcher, 1989.

McWhirter, Norris, and Ross McWhirter. *Illustrated Encyclopedia of Facts.* Doubleday, 1969.

Maisel, Eric. *Staying Sane in the Arts.* Tarcher, 1992.

Malazesta, Carol Zander. *Psychology and Aging.* Academic Press, 1990.

Maxmen, Jerrold. *The New Psychiatry.* William Morrow, 1985.

Maybruck, Patricia. *Pregnancy & Dreams.* Tarcher, 1989.

Morin, Jack. "The Four Corners of Eroticism." In *The Erotic Impulse,* ed. David Steinberg. Tarcher, 1992.

Murphy, Michael. *The Future of the Body.* Tarcher, 1992.

Nelson, John. *Healing the Split.* Tarcher, 1992.

Ornstein, Robert. *The Psychology of Consciousness.* Penguin, 1975.

Patzer, Gordon. *The Physical Attractiveness Phenomenon.* Plenum, 1985.

Pauker, Samuel L., and Miriam Arond. *The First Year of Marriage: What to Expect, What to Accept, and What You Can Change.* Warner, 1987.

Penfield, Wilder. *The Mystery of the Mind: A Critical Study of Consciousness and the Human Brain.* Princeton University Press, 1975.

Plutchik, Robert. *Emotions: A Psychoevolutionary Synthesis*. Harper, 1980.

Report of the Committee on the Operation of the British Sexual Containment Act, 1978.

Ring, Kenneth. *Heading Toward Omega: The Near Death Experience*. Morrow, 1985.

Robinson, Daniel. *The Enlightened Machine: An Analytical Introduction to Neuropsychology*. Dickenson, 1973.

Robson, Elizabeth, and Gwenyth Edwards. *Getting Help: A Woman's Guide to Therapy*. E. P. Dutton, 1980.

Rossi, Ernest. *Dreams and the Development of Personality*. Brunner, 1985.

———. *The Psychobiology of Mind-Body Healing*. Norton, 1986.

———. *The 20-Minute Break: The New Science of Ultradian Rhythms*. Tarcher, 1989.

Sagan, Carl. *The Dragons of Eden: Speculations on the Origin of Human Intelligence*. Random House, 1977.

Saurez, Rick, Roger Mills, and Darlene Stewart. *Sanity, Insanity and Commonsense*. Ballantine Books, 1987.

Schultz, Dwayne. *Freud and Jung: Intimate Friends, Dangerous Rivals*. Tarcher, 1990.

Schwartz, Bernard. *When the Body Speaks Its Mind*. Putnam, 1993.

Siegel, Alan. *Dreams That Can Change Your Life*. Tarcher, 1991.

Simonton, Dean K. "Creativity and Wisdom in Aging." In *Handbook of the Psychology of Aging*, ed. James Birren and Warner Schaie.

———. *Genius, Creativity, and Leadership*. Harvard University Press, 1983.

Singer, Jerome. *The Inner World of Daydreaming*. Harper, 1975.

Singer, Jerome, and J. S. Antrobus, eds. *The Stream of Consciousness*. Academic Press, 1973.

Smith, Adam. *Powers of the Mind*. Summit, 1982.

Starker, Steven. *F-States: The Power of Fantasy in Human Creativity*. Newcastle, 1985.

Stone, Sandy. "The Empire Strikes Back." In *Body Guards*, edited by Julie Epstein and Karen Straub. Rutledge, 1989.

Strupp, Hans. *Psychotherapy for Better or Worse: The Problem of Negative Effects*. Aronson, 1977.

Talbot, Michael. *The Holographic Universe*. Harper, 1991.

Tessina, Tina. *Lovestyles*. Newcastle, 1987.

———. *The Thirteenth Step*. Tarcher, 1991.

Trivers, Robert L. *Social Evolution*. Benjamin/Cummings, 1985.

U.S. Military Academy at West Point. Office of Physical Education. "Report on the Admission of Women to the U.S. Military Academy."

Department of Behavioral Science and Leadership. U.S. Military Academy at West Point, 1979.

Walsh, Roger. *The Spirit of Shamanism.* Tarcher, 1991.

Watson, Lyall. *Super Nature.* Bantam, 1974.

Webster, Paula. "Eroticism and Taboo." In *The Erotic Impulse*, ed. David Steinberg. Tarcher, 1992.

Wilson, Glenn. *Love and Instinct.* Temple Smith, 1981.

Woolis, Rebecca. *When Someone You Love Has a Mental Illness.* Tarcher, 1993.

Zilbergeld, Bernie. *The Shrinking of America.* Little, Brown, 1983.

Periodicals

Readers interested in more information on the topics included in this book may want to consult the following publications:

American Journal of Psychiatry, Archives of General Psychiatry, Archives of Sexual Behavior, Archives of the Third International Congress of Sexologists, Atlantic Monthly, Children and Play, Cognitive Psychology, Developmental Psychology, Dimensions of Physical Attractiveness, Discover, First, Glamour, Harper's, Hospital and Community Psychiatry, Human Behavior, Human Factors, Journal of Aging and Human Development, Journal of Behavioral Medicine, Journal of Clinical Psychology, Journal of Experimental Psychology, Journal of Marital and Family Therapy, Journal of Nervous and Mental Disease, Journal of Personality and Social Psychology, Journal of Personality Assessment, Journal of Sex and Marital Therapists, Journal of Social and Biological Structures, Journal of Social Psychology, Journal of the American Medical Association, Ladies Home Journal, Los Angeles Reader, Los Angeles Times, Macleans, Mademoiselle, McCall's, Motivation and Emotion, National Geographic, New England Journal of Medicine, New York Times, Newsweek, Parents, Perceptual and Motor Skills, Physiological Psychology, Prevention, Proceedings of the National Academy of Sciences, Psychology, Psychology Today, Redbook, Science, Science News, Scientific American, Social Evolution, Teen, Time, U.S. News & World Report, Western Journal of Speech Communication, Woman's Day.

Index

About the Authors

JEAN STINE has ghostwritten a number of best-selling celebrity biographies and self-help books. As a journalist, Jean has sold more than 1,000 stories to publications such as the *Washington Post*, the *Los Angeles News, Movieline, Eros*, and *Amazing Stories*, and has been syndicated in every major daily newspaper in America. For more than a decade Jean served as editor-in-chief of a number of publishers including the Donning Co., Rainbow Publications, and Jeremy P. Tarcher.

CAMDEN BENARES is a former magazine editor and free-lance journalist with hundreds of articles to his credit. In addition he is the author of best-selling books such as *Zen Without Zen Masters, A Handful of Zen* and *Common Sense Tarot*.